Alison Johnson grew up in Aberdeen and gained her first
degree, an MA in Medieval and Renaissance English,
at Aberdeen University. After picking up a second degree
at Oxford, she married Andrew Johnson and moved with
him back to Scotland where they both found jobs as
teachers on the Isle of Harris. On the west coast of the
island they found Scarista House, a decaying manse which
they converted into one of the most highly acclaimed
hotels in Scotland, which receives yearly accolades from
all the major hotel guides.

Alison Johnson is the author of A HOUSE BY THE
SHORE, in which she describes the 12-year struggle
to turn the derelict Scarista House into an
award-winning restaurant and hotel.

Also by Alison Johnson and published by Futura:
A HOUSE BY THE SHORE

SCARISTA STYLE

*A free-range and humane approach
to cooking and eating*
by
ALISON JOHNSON

Futura

A Futura Book

First published in Great Britain in 1987
by Victor Gollancz Ltd, London

This edition published in 1988 by Futura Publications, a Division
of Macdonald & Co (Publishers) Ltd, London & Sydney.

ISBN 0 7088 3737 9

Printed and bound in Great Britain by
The Guernsey Press Co. Ltd, Guernsey, Channel Islands

Futura Publications
A Division of
Macdonald & Co (Publishers) Ltd
Greater London House
Hampstead Road
London NW1 7QX

A member of Maxwell Pergamon Publishing Corporation plc

Contents

Shellfish   68

Game and other Meat   80

Cereals and Vegetable Side-dishes   94

CONTENTS

About the Athene Trust and Compassion in World Farming

The copyright and author's income from this book have been given to the Athene Trust, which has been set up to further the educational work of Compassion in World Farming.

CIWF is an organisation formed to oppose the exploitation of animals and land in modern agricultural practice. In the past thirty years, factory farming has become very big business. Vast numbers of meat animals are mass-produced in cruelly confined conditions. To feed them, the most fertile farmlands are constantly overcropped to produce cereals and oilseeds. It is the belief of CIWF that the only sane policy is to reduce reliance on animal protein, use our best croplands to produce food for direct human consumption, and realign the research and expertise now devoted to intensive animal husbandry towards less wasteful production.

The Athene Trust is designed with young people in mind, to provide information through schools and educational establishments, by means of project packs, films and so on. But young or old, we all need educating. It is easy for us, as consumers, to hide from the ugly facts of factory farming. The animals are shut away in windowless sheds, where we cannot see, hear, or smell their suffering. There is plenty food for us to buy in the shops, so we need never find out that the other face of our wasteful Western plenty is Third World famine. CIWF aims to make plain to consumers the twin immoralities of large scale animal abuse and wastage of global resources inherent in modern agriculture, and to publicise alternatives. Their message is "Don't buy your food in ignorance", and so is mine.

If you would like further information about the work of the Athene Trust and CIWF you can contact them at 20 Lavant Street, Petersfield, Hampshire, GU32 3EW.

Introduction

When I telephone suppliers for the first time, and say I am speaking from Harris, they nearly always repeat "Paris", knowledgeably.

"No, H-arris!"

"Harris? where's that?"

If you look at the top left-hand corner of a map of Britain, you may see Harris. On some maps, it is put in a box, or missed out altogether. Scarista is on its western side, looking out across the empty Atlantic.

We bought Scarista House as a dismal semi-ruin ten years ago. After an enjoyable do-it-yourself conversion period, I retreated to the kitchen and Andrew sallied out front, and we opened our doors as an hotel. We were "noticed" immediately by some of the major hotel guides, which was just as well, since we had no money and few customers. Inflated with righteous pride, we set high standards. We bought ingredients with regard to quality, not price, and I cooked (and still cook) in a last minute frenzy, to ensure freshness.

For the first few years that was the challenge, to produce food of excellent quality in an unlikely location: and unlikely it is, for we are fifty-five miles from the nearest supermarket, and home-grown vegetables blow away as often as they take root in our breezy garden. We availed ourselves of the fine local venison and seafood, built up a network of suppliers, and eschewed all processed imitations of real food. Gradually, tins and packets were edged out of the larder. Last to go were chicken stock cubes. We noticed our dog would snort in disgust at gravy containing even a crumb of them. We respected his judgment: really, they did taste a bit odd. But then chicken tasted a bit odd. And having got this particular oddness up our noses, there was a certain something about duck . . . and pork . . . and bacon. Not to put too fine a point on it, "*Ça sent la merde*"; each animal's flesh was faintly permeated with the odour of its own dung. Why? Had they been rolling in it? Penned up in the fumes of it?

We had heard of factory farming, but it is pleasanter to forget about it. When we actually began to enquire, we found that the life and death of our poultry and pigs was even more gruesome than our suspicions had suggested. When we knew enough to be unable to forget it any longer, we excluded totally all intensively farmed meat and eggs from our kitchen, together with the worst productions of cruel rearing methods or inhumane slaughter. We have never regretted it or found the new regime hard to manage. We use less animal protein and a greater variety of fruit and vegetables than before, and the proportion of shellfish and game has risen. No animal remains are wasted now: I pressure cook all fish trimmings with vegetable peelings into a delectable goo for the hens, our dog dines off the toughest portions of meat, and the seagulls have all the fat and kipper skins. Our reputation for fine food has not suffered. We can feed people well and imaginatively at dinner with only one dish containing meat or fish, and the rest of the courses built upon fresh fruit and vegetables, free range eggs and farmhouse cheeses. More and more people want to come, and our profits have not decreased: in other words, it is perfectly possible to run a hotel and restaurant business on these lines, and it should certainly not be more difficult to do so with an ordinary household.

But why bother, if food is convenient and a good bargain, and you haven't yet smelt the dung in it? Why look for trouble? Certainly, the giants of the processing, packaging and marketing world will do everything possible to keep you blindfolded. Their wares are appetisingly clean and neat: their wrappings are bucolically cheerful with dancing pigs and flowery milkmaids, chirpy chickens and thatched cottages. But these are elaborate lies designed to conceal squalid realities.

Let's start at the luxury end of the market. Take, for example, the hygienic package of frog's legs you can buy in a delicatessen: "cuisses de grenouilles" in a smart restaurant. The cuisses, delicately sauced upon your plate, were probably sliced from a living frog in Bangladesh. The head, body and pathetically groping forelegs were left to die slowly: one death for every two legs on the plate. To compound the evil, these frogs used to keep down insect pests for human farmers in the famine-stricken areas where they are caught. No frogs now—so the farmers turn to the chemical insecticides, many such as DDT and dieldrin long since banned in the rich West, and cynically exported to more desperate markets. They poison people and wildlife as well as insects: that is why we have got rid of them here. So what is the answer? Don't eat frog's legs, say compassion and common sense. Farm frogs for gourmets, cries ingenious greed.

My claim is that we should only eat what we could bear to see killed before dinner. If you could not eat frog's legs while frog's bodies dragged themselves painfully round your table—don't eat frog's legs. Remember, too, that nicely breaded scampi were the tails pulled from living langoustines, and that the crab claws all folksy and tartan in a west highland dining room were wrenched off a living body.

Don't be misled by the red-herring of cold-bloodedness. We have no proof at all that cold-blooded creatures don't feel pain. A creature that did not have sensation would not flee from danger. There is every evidence that frogs, fish and crustaceans are sensitive to touch: and such sensitivity cannot be disassociated from pain. Don't listen to pseudo-scientific nonsense about "flight reactions" and "negative stimuli". Human beings have a flight reaction too, if threatened with the negative stimulus of a red-hot poker.

In any case, the warm-blooded fare no better at human hands. You may forgo the cuisses de grenouilles and plump for the pâté de foie gras. Plump is right: the stuff is 55% fat—deliberately diseased by the disgusting practice of *gavage*, force-feeding geese up to 6½ lb (3 kg) of salty, fatty maize in a day. The goose is restrained—it may have its feet nailed to the floor, or be sat on by a fat grandmother, traditionally: in more modern and even more fiendish circumstances, it is held fast in a brace and attached to a hellish engine worked by a foot-pedal, which simultaneously stretches its neck, forces its gullet open, and pumps the maize down its throat. An elastic band round its neck prevents it vomiting the food up again. This isn't a scene from a nasty video: it happens every day to millions of birds like those you may have watched with pleasure waddling round an old-fashioned farm, or flying overhead with haunting cries in autumn and early spring. Think about it before ordering any Strasbourg pâté next Christmas. And while in that restaurant, don't have the escalope of veal, it is tender and pale because the animal was deliberately deprived of exercise and iron. To produce white veal, the calves are kept from a few days old to slaughter in individual crates 24 in (60 cm) wide. In other words, they can't turn round even to groom themselves. They can't touch or see their fellows, far less play or run about. The floors of their pens are slatted wood, without straw, because if they had straw they would eat it in a desperate search for roughage, which ruminants require. Instead they are kept on an all-liquid diet, to produce the flabby pale flesh said to be desired by the consumer. There is in fact a humane British system of veal-raising, where calves are kept in small groups in straw covered yards. But their flesh is not pallid enough for the gourmet market: hence about ninety per cent of the veal sold in restaurants—any veal that is pale—comes from the inhumane crate system. True, a lot of it is imported from France and Holland, but no room for congratulation here: great numbers of British calves are sent, often at a few days old, by road to the continent, as far south as Italy, destined for crate-rearing. Their wretched journey can take 48 hours, without rest or food. Anyone who has seen a new-born calf can imagine their miseries.

Well, not many of us have frequent access to such doubtful luxuries as foie gras and white veal. But what about those cheap and convenient forms of protein, the chicken and the egg? Chickens—and turkeys and ducks—are reared crammed together in huge, dim, warm sheds, where they will not waste valuable feed by exercising. Feeding and watering is automatic. Almost the only human touch is to remove corpses and cull runtish birds. When the flock is full grown, they are stuffed into crates, with considerably less care than a market gardener stows his cabbages, often sustaining broken wings and legs. The crates are piled into a lorry, and moved to the slaughterhouse. If you are driving in a city or on a motorway very early in the morning, you may end up behind one of these ghastly loads—feathers and the odd wing or leg sticking out between the slats of the crates. Don't try to forget the sight—try to remember it. These weren't feather dusters, but live birds: and their next torment is to be hung upside down on a conveyor belt, stunned, bled and dipped in boiling water. Most are dead by the boiling water stage, but not all. Slightly larger or smaller birds can miss the automatic stunner and knife and be scalded alive. So your chicken may be half-boiled before it ever gets in the bag. That is the life and death of your country-fresh, down-home style, happy valley chicken—or turkey, or duck, or nowadays even quail or partridge.

And eggs? Worse and worse. Ninety per cent of British eggs come from battery units, where laying pullets are crammed sometimes five or even six to a wire cage 18 in × 20 in (45 × 50 cm) for their whole miserable lives, day and night. They cannot perch, scratch, dustbathe or even stretch their wings. They often lose their feathers—they don't need them, the producers explain, in the warm battery house. If they are released from the cages, they can't stand or walk: they don't need legs either, to be egg-laying machines. Lay they must: they are specially bred for that ability, and contrary to popular myth, ovulation does not cease because of mental or physical deprivation. If it did there would be no human famine in Ethiopia and elsewhere, for when life became too wretched, people would be unable to breed; convenient if true—but not true, either for people or hens. So don't assume with Mother Katherine of the Convent of the Order of the Passion of Jesus, which keeps a very intensive battery egg unit near Daventry that "if they weren't happy they wouldn't lay so many eggs". Eggs may be obscenely mislabelled—fresh farm eggs, country eggs. Supermarkets may feature photographs of straw nests harbouring a homely clutch. But unless the box is clearly marked "free range", don't be fooled. I would also say, unless it is labelled "free range", don't buy it. Free range will cost pennies more—probably no more than 20p per dozen. For an average family, the money you might save on buying hell's eggs will get you, in a year, the cost of a new hair-do or a couple of bottles of gin. And if you are visiting that French restaurant again, forget the quail's eggs. These days they, too, are produced in battery conditions.

Once you have your free-range eggs, what about the bacon to go with them? The outlook is poor. Don't buy Danish, that's for sure: and if you buy British, you won't do much better. About sixty per cent of the nation's pigs are intensively housed. This means that the pregnant sows are permanently penned on concrete, usually without straw, and without room to turn. These are the infamous "dry sow stalls". In the farrowing crate, piglets have a separate compartment from which they can reach the confined sow's teats—indeed, she cannot escape from them for an instant. The sow's only relief from imprisonment is when she is put to the boar to be served: then the whole life-in-death cycle begins again. For millions of pigs there is never a chance to root or wallow, or to interact with others of their kind. Pigs are intelligent animals, particularly prone to boredom and stress. To alleviate boredom, they gnaw the bars of their cages. As for stress, they sometimes die of it on their way to the slaughterhouse, or if they don't die of it the signs of suffering are evident in unusually pallid, rather wet meat. The worst is discarded, presumably made into pork pies, but some of it finds its way into the shops: I know I have handled pork like that before I realised what caused it. If you can buy local pork and bacon in an area where you actually see numerous pigs rooting in the fields, you are in luck; but if you haven't seen a pig for years fear the worst: it is probably the truth.

And the rot keeps spreading. In the south, you are seeing more and more "Scotch salmon". It is farmed from the stripped eggs of that magnificent wild Atlantic fish, with its intense migratory instinct. The fish are reared entirely in net cages, so close crammed that when ready for "harvest" there are 10 per cubic metre. To prevent the flesh becoming too flabby the cages may be placed in a current so that the fish have to swim constantly to avoid being crushed against the cage wall.

Nothing is getting better for the animals we eat. If you see rabbit meat, it will probably be hutch-reared: and modern "hutches" are bare mesh cages without litter. Pheasants may have been reared in pens, fitted with metal bits or painfully debeaked to prevent their boredom finding an outlet in feather-pecking. Red deer are being farmed now —as yet fairly humanely, but for how long? Much beef in America and more and more in this country is being reared in feed-lots and barns, cramped together and fed on concentrates. Experiments are afoot to see if there is profit in cage-bred lamb.

There is big money in all this: big money and little employment. It takes few workers to monitor the automatically fed, watered, warmed and ventilated stock in the windowless factory farms. True, the intended automation may fail, so that beasts starve, freeze or suffocate: if fire breaks out, they may often burn to death. But what does it matter? The law has not been broken, and insurance covers losses. There are government codes of practice which appear to offer minimal protection to intensively farmed livestock, but these codes are constantly flouted, and never enforced.

The only way the consumer can beat the system is not to buy the products of it, however it is dressed up in pretty packaging, with smiling cows, contented hens, and flowers and trees. It is not only the oven-ready chickens and veal cutlets that come under suspicion, but all the processed foods and ready meals containing battery-farmed products. Stock cubes—canned soups—pet food—made-up pies and pâtés: all these make the profit margins worthwhile for the big producers. Read the list of ingredients carefully: if you are not put off by the first five or six, which are probably chemicals, look hard at the next, which may be "chicken".

Consider dairy produce carefully, too. The dairy cow, comparatively speaking, does not have a bad life. She is a sensitive creature, and lactation can be considerably reduced by stress, so it doesn't pay to torment her. Most cross-bred calves are reared for beef, and if they are grass-reared that is not as bad a fate as some animals suffer. Other dairy calves of pure breed are slaughtered at a few days old. But the less lucky are sold to the crated veal industry. Veal is simply a by-product of dairying.

Any reader who has not given up by now on this catalogue of abuses is probably feeling depressed. What is there left to eat? Is it worth bothering, when so much is wrong? Certainly, it is worth it. There are degrees of evil in the system: I would put battery egg production lowest of the low, of the common abuses, and regard dairy produce with ambivalence, but these are personal judgements. *The important thing is to make judgements at all.* Even in the crazed world of EEC quotas, ultimately demand must decide supply. It may take a long time, but if consumers simply do not buy the products of intensive farming, the monolithic indifference of governments will be shaken. Either the product will fade from the scene, or more humane methods of production will be found: in many cases, such methods are already known. Eventually, laws are changed in line with public opinion. Switzerland is phasing out the battery cage by 1991; in West Germany, the state of Hessen has taken up and enforced a Federal ruling that such cages are illegal; in Holland, 13 per cent of eggs come from "scratching hens". In this country, legislation is on its way to phase out the veal crate by 1990. Small victories, but significant.

As consumers, we all have the power to change things, by thinking before buying. Of course the choice of animal protein is then narrowed —you eat less of it—maybe none of it—but this is no bad thing. Quite apart from the misery of the animals concerned, there are other arguments. The health factor is well known, in spite of the meat trade's attempts to suppress it. Everyone is aware by now that the too carnivorous suffer more of every ailment from cancer to acne. Not quite so well known is the terrible waste of grain, pulse and fish protein—up to nine tenths wastage—in producing meat, especially beef, poultry and pork. In a world where many people are starving, everyone in the rich west must take responsibility for that. In 1984 we imported about £1½ million worth of oilseed for animal feed from the farmland of Ethiopia. Even less publicised is the export of the techniques and apparatus of intensive animal husbandry to third world countries, fostering not only animal abuse but the very waste of vegetable proteins and human health these methods have produced in the west. Least considered of all, perhaps, is the massive destruction of wildlife habitat caused by our flesh eating propensities. Tropical forests are axed to make way for the Great American Steak; nearer home, sophisticated fishing gear nets not only the fish, but the egg and larval stages of many species, thousands of sea birds, seals, and "non-commercial species"—and all this often for fish meal, to feed the intensively-kept meat animals.

Knowing what you are eating, I think, is enough to achieve a reduction in animal abuse. The mere facts, pondered on, remove the desire for excessive animal protein. But habit is not so easy to break. We are used to bacon and eggs, meat and two veg, pâté sandwiches, sausage rolls. How on earth do you plan a special dinner party? What can you offer weekend guests for breakfast? There are, of course, plenty of vegetarian cookery books, but not everyone wants to be a vegetarian. In fact, a sudden switch can be traumatic and discouraging: once, in days when I was more carnivorous and more orthodox, I gave up meat for Lent, and thought about nothing but steaks for forty days and forty nights. In recent years, I have given up Lent, and steaks. But I still cook for non-vegetarians. The recipes which follow can, I hope, be used by people of both persuasions. Outside the main course sections, hardly anything contains meat or fish, and many of the second section can be used as vegetarian main dishes. At the end you will find some dinner menus. If you try them, I hope you will be impressed by their lightness and balance, rather than depressed by the lack of truffled pâté and quails' eggs.

And for those who have borne patiently with me this far, and are still thinking longingly of roast dinners, here is the heart-cry of a fellow sufferer:

A priest once tried to teach a wolf his letters . . .
"A", said the priest, starting the rule.
"A", said the wolf, who was no fool.
"B", said the priest, "Say that with me!"
"B", said the wolf, "I do agree."
"C", said the priest, "Do carry on!"
"C", said the wolf. "When will this be done?"
The priest replied: "You say it through!"
The wolf said: "That I cannot do."
"Then spell out the sounds from any name!"
"LAMB!" said the wolf. "LAMB! LAMB! LAMB! LAMB!"
The priest observed the sense of this.
Wolf's mouth spelled out Wolf's thoughts.*

* From *Medieval Fables of Marie de France*, translated by Jeanette Beer (Dragon's World, 1981).

A Note on Serving Quantities

The recipes in this book are designed to serve 6 amply as part of a full meal, unless otherwise stated. The exceptions are to be found among the Appetisers and Cereal and Vegetable Side Dishes, which will serve 6 in those capacities, or 2–4 as a vegetarian main course, where suitable.

A Note on Oven Temperatures

I am exceptionally vague about cooking temperatures. I have a very old Aga which alternately sulks and rages. Also an electric cooker: our electricity supply travels a long way over the mountains from Stornaway and comes in three varieties—too much, too little and none at all. So I am seldom in a position to cook things for 7½ minutes at 185°C. Where accuracy is desirable for a particular recipe, I have put a Centigrade temperature in the text (with its Fahrenheit equivalent). Likewise if preheating is essential to the success of a dish, I have mentioned it. For those lucky cooks with well-behaved ovens, I append a scale of equivalent temperatures.

	°C	°F	Regulo
Very slow	115–135	240–280	¼–½
Slow	135–160	280–320	1
Very moderate	160–170	320–340	3
Moderate	170–185	340–370	4
Moderately hot	185–205	370–400	5–6
Hot	205–225	400–440	7
Very hot	225–250	440–480	8–9

Soups

Don't you like our turtle soup? No!
Throw it out the old front door.

Thus sang Ivor Cutler soulfully, and since I hold firmly to the conservationist party line on turtle abuse, I cannot but agree with the forceful negative. The implied waste in the follow-up, however, shocks me to the core. Soup is by its very nature the most rewardingly frugal and nourishing of foods, as you cook all the ingredients together, losing none of the flavour or nutrients. Soup in one form or another is the mainstay of delicate convalescents and hearty peasants, tender infants and toothless elders. Queen Henrietta Maria started each day with "a good porringer full" of hen broth. Alexis Soyer revitalised the Parisian poor with wholesome brews of unpeeled vegetables.

At Scarista I serve soup about five days out of seven as a first or second course. This is not actually for any of the reasons expressed in the above eulogy, but because we possess twenty-three soup-cups and only fifty-two small flat plates. If we use most of these for the first two courses, there's an awful lot of washing-up to be done before anyone can have cheese or pudding. Inevitably, someone (not *me*) has put them in the dishwasher, so that they are unappetisingly hot and soapy when required for the chocolate mousse. That may be a poor reason for serving soup often, but it's what is known as a secret of the trade.

Carrots provide thickening without the addition of flour, forming a light, aromatic base, which supports fruit and herbs well. These combinations are a good start to a rich meal, offering the cleanness of a salad even in climatic conditions that would make salad eaters turn blue.

Apricot and Carrot Soup

Use only the sourest type of apricot. The more wizened and shabby they look, the better, for savoury dishes. They will resemble biltong to start with, but in quarter of an hour they will be plump and perfumed.

2 oz (50 g) dried apricots
1½ oz (40 g) butter
3 medium carrots, coarsely grated
1 medium onion, finely chopped
½-inch (1.25 cm) piece of
    cinnamon stick
a pinch of dried basil
salt and sugar to taste
1 pt (570 ml) water

Stew the apricots in the water till tender, and liquidise. Melt the butter, put in the cinnamon, and add the carrots and onion as you get them ready. Do not brown this mixture. Add the basil and the apricot purée. Simmer till the vegetables are tender.

Add salt and sugar to taste—get the balance right or it will taste dreadful, but properly seasoned it is teasingly aromatic.

Carrot and Orange Soup

1 lb (450 g) carrots
½ lb (225 g) onions
2 oz (50 g) butter
3-inch (7.5 cm) strip of orange peel
1 pt (570 ml) water
salt
juice of 1 large orange

Cut up the onion and carrots roughly. Remove the orange peel very thinly, without pith: a carrot peeler is ideal for this job.

Put everything except the orange juice in a pan and simmer, covered, for about half an hour. Liquidise or sieve. Add the orange juice, test for salt and reheat, but don't reboil or the delicate scent of orange will disappear.

Kail and Oatmeal Soup

Curly Kail is one of the few vegetables I can grow easily. It is daunting to caterpillars, unappetising to rabbits, impervious to rain. It thrives on frost and snow. Eventually winter gales finish it off, but it puts up a fight first. Not much wonder it is a traditional vegetable in the North of Scotland. Scottish vegetable gardens used to be called "kailyards": kail being any of the cabbage family, but typically Curly Kail, defiantly tough and green in all weathers. Kail and oatmeal is a time-honoured combination. "Kail Brose" was made by stirring raw oatmeal into the boiling liquor strained from cooked kail: a dour and economical dish to keep farm labourers labouring diligently at little expense. This soup is a slightly more sophisticated version.

> about 1 lb (450 g) curly kail
> 2 large onions
> 3 oz (75 g) butter
> 3 oz (75 g) medium oatmeal
> salt
> about 1½ pt (825 ml) water

If the kail leaves are large, cut out the ribs. If the leaves are small use the ribs too; you will then only need ¾ lb (350 g). Shred the kail across in ¼-inch (6 mm) strips.

Chop the onion, not too fine, and fry in 2 oz (50 g) of the butter till just beginning to brown. Stir in 2 oz (50 g) of the oatmeal, the kail, the water and salt. Simmer for 15 minutes, stirring occasionally, as oatmeal tends to collect in the bottom of the pan and stick.

Meanwhile, fry the remaining meal in the rest of the butter till it turns pale and slightly crisp. Add a little salt and a lot of freshly ground pepper. Dish the soup with the fried meal sprinkled on top. You can add cream before dishing if you want a richer soup.

Cauliflowers are another useful soup vegetable. A classic cream of cauliflower will only be as good as the cauliflower was fresh, but if you have to deal with execrable objects looking fit only for the compost heap, you can still produce interesting flavours by adding some strong-tasting complement. The first example is unashamedly à l'Indienne. The other combination was suggested by Rhoda, our butcher's office lady, when fennel first appeared in Hebridean shops. To persuade her family that the exotic new arrival was edible, she had cooked it along with the more familiar cauliflower, and it was delicious, she told me. She was quite right.

Spicy Cauliflower Soup

Ready-ground spices are all right for the discreet touches required in baking or in Middle Eastern cookery, but they are no good at all for a dish which relies on spicing for its main impact. However, grinding in a pestle and mortar is very laborious. I recommend using an old coffee grinder. Don't bother trying to get the mix too fine unless you are the sort of person who screams at a tomato seed. If you only have one coffee grinder, you can still risk using it occasionally for spices: but wipe it out AT ONCE with a lightly oiled piece of kitchen paper, then a dry piece: then put a tablespoon of kitchen salt into the grinder and switch it on for its maximum time. Do this two or three times, empty it, and wipe it out again. Dried pomegranate seeds can sometimes be had from Pakistani or Indian grocers, but if you can't get them, omit them, and grate a small tart apple in with the ginger.

For the soup
2 teaspoons coriander seeds
1 teaspoon cumin seeds
½ teaspoon black peppercorns
½ teaspoon turmeric
2 teaspoons dried pomegranate
    seeds
2 oz (50 g) butter
1 large onion fairly finely chopped
1-inch (2.5 cm) piece of fresh
    ginger, grated
2 cloves of garlic, crushed
1 cauliflower pulled into small sprigs
1 pt (570 ml) water
salt to taste
juice of ½ to 1 lemon

For the garnish:
½ oz (15 g) butter
1 oz (25 g) coarsely chopped
  blanched almonds
1 teaspoon paprika
(1 teaspoon sesame seeds
  —optional)
(1 teaspoon poppy seeds
  —optional)

Grind the first five ingredients and fry them in the butter for about one minute. Add the onion, ginger and garlic, and fry for another few minutes. Put in the cauliflower, add water, and about 1 level teaspoon of salt. Stir well and simmer till very tender—about 20 minutes. Liquidise about half the mixture, and return it to the pan, leaving the rest rough. Add lemon juice and extra water if necessary, but leave it fairly thick. Reheat without boiling. Fry the almonds and paprika in the ½ oz (15 g) of butter. You can add a spoonful of poppy seeds or sesame seeds if you like. Scatter this mixture on each serving of soup.

Cauliflower and Fennel Soup

Don't overcook this: any of the cabbage family tastes much too cabbagey if boiled for long.

1 small cauliflower
an equal weight of fennel
1 medium onion
2 oz (50 g) butter
¾ pt (425 ml) water
up to ½ pt (275 ml) cream
juice of 1 lemon
salt to taste

Save some of the best feathery leaves of the fennel. Chop finely and set aside.

Slice the remaining vegetables roughly and put in a pan with the butter and stew gently till the onion loses its crispness. Cover with water. Simmer for 10 minutes. Liquidise, adding more water if necessary to make a thick purée.

Add the lemon juice, cream and salt to taste, then reheat without boiling. Garnish with the chopped fennel leaves.

Kailkenny Soup

"Kailkenny" is an uncompromisingly grim Scottish dish of mashed potatoes and long-boiled cabbage. But since it is a pretty name, I appropriated it for this soup, as sounding more enticing than sprout-and-potato. You can use nasty old sprouts for this, as long as you take care to cut away all the dingy ochre and slimy black bits on the outside, and wash away the taint of these unpleasantnesses before proceeding further.

1 lb (450 g) potatoes	1 pt (570 ml) water
1 lb (450 g) brussels sprouts	½ pt (275 ml) creamy milk or
2 medium onions	cream
2 oz (50 g) butter	salt, pepper and nutmeg

Prepare the sprouts, peel the potatoes and cut them into slices, chop the onions. Turn the vegetables in the melting butter, add water and simmer till just tender—not more than 15 minutes, or the sprouts will taste sulphurous. Liquidise, add milk or cream, and season to taste. Serve with croûtons and a sprinkling of chopped chives or parsley.

Lovage and Celery Soup

You will be glad of this recipe if you grow lovage, as it will have taken over your garden and you won't know what to do with it. "The root grows thick, great and deep, spreading much and enduring long . . . It is planted in gardens, where it grows large," says Culpeper blandly, adding that "a decoction of the root is a remedy for ague." If you don't live in a malarial marsh, you will find you have a large surplus of this particular herb.

This is one of my favourite soups, and worth suffering the rampages of the plant for.

2 medium onions	3 large handfuls lovage leaves
1 head celery	¾ pt (425 ml) water
2 large potatoes	½ pt (275 ml) milk
2 oz (50 g) butter	¼ pt (150 ml) cream

Chop the onion, celery and potatoes coarsely and sweat them in the butter for a few minutes. Add the water and lovage and bring to the boil. Cover and simmer till the vegetables are very soft. Stir it occasionally, as the mixture will be thick and inclined to stick.

The soup now has to be sieved, as celery is hairy stuff. It is easier to do this if you liquidise it first, adding the milk as you do so.

Return the soup to the pan, add salt to taste and the cream. Reheat without boiling. Serve with a blob of cream or some freshly chopped lovage on top.

Tomato and Sweet Pepper Soup

It seems to have become an old cookery wives' tale that tinned tomatoes are preferable in flavour to all but the best in true Brit. type tomatoes. Certainly the sickly-hued November "fresh" item in the shops tastes of very little. Here it differs from the bright red tinned version, which tastes of very little but tin. Tinned tomatoes, in my opinion, are fine in a dish with other flavours stronger than tin—strong spices, red wine, or half a sack of onions will usually overcome. But for a fresh-tasting vegetable soup, you should use raw tomatoes. I concede, however, that a teaspoon or so of tomato purée and a good pinch of sugar will give body to the more aqueously underripe, without tasting suspect. In the recipe below, red peppers seem to ripen the flavour of tomatoes without recourse to canning. To get rid of tomato skins and seeds, I prefer to cook everything together in large chunks, then liquidise and sieve. That way no flavour is lost. You could get the same result by chopping finely before cooking and sieving. I don't advise blanching and seeding for this tomato recipe.

For the soup:	For the garnish:
2 medium onions	1 tablespoon yoghurt
2 medium red peppers	1 tablespoon cream
1½ lb (675 g) tomatoes	a little salt
1½ oz (40 g) butter	paprika or freshly chopped green
1½ oz (40 g) flour	herbs (parsley, mint or
1 pt (570 ml) water	marjoram)
salt and pepper	

Cut up the vegetables coarsely. Make a light roux with the flour and butter and add the vegetables. Stir in the water, and cook till just tender—the onion and pepper should not have gone soggy, though. Liquidise the mixture and then press it through a sieve, season to taste and reheat. For the garnish, mix the yoghurt and cream with a pinch of salt. Put a blob of this in each serving, and a scattering of red or green over that.

Nettle Soup

It is such a fiddle picking nettles that I hardly ever make this soup, which is a pity as it is distinctive and delicious. You can wear rubber gloves to pick and wash nettles, but being too impatient for that I usually just grab them and curse. Grasp a nettle by its stem and it will flick back up your sleeve and sting your wrist. Jump back swearing and its sister will get you in the back of the knees.

young nettle shoots to fill a 2-pint (1.2-litre) jug, loosely packed
1 medium onion
2 oz (50 g) butter
2 oz (50 g) wholemeal flour

a 2-inch (5 cm) strip of lemon rind
1¼ pt (700 ml) water
salt, black pepper, nutmeg and lemon juice to taste

Wash the nettles—they collect earth and bits of grass. Chop the onion finely and sauté in the butter. Stir in the flour and then the nettles and water. Simmer, but not for too long or the nettles will lose their fresh colour. The onion can afford to be slightly crisp in this soup.

You can either liquidise everything, if you want a smooth soup, or leave it as it is, providing your nettles were in small pieces to start with. I prefer to liquidise half and mix it back in—this gives the most intense flavour without losing the interesting texture. Season to taste. You can add cream if you like it.

Orkney Soup

I don't know if this soup originates in the Orkneys at all. I think it is probably rather like Steak Bonnie Prince Charlie or Robert the Bruce's Spider Cookies, but leaving the Romance of Scotland aside, it is an unusually flavoured yet immediately appealing dish. I have found it very popular.

2 carrots
a chunk of swede or turnip—about 4 oz (100 g)
3 stalks celery
3 medium onions
2 or 3 leeks and/or a few green cabbage leaves

1 oz (25 g) butter
2 tablespoons oatmeal (pinhead is best)
1½ pt (825 ml) stock
½ pt (275 ml) milk
chopped parsley

Chop all the vegetables fairly fine. The leeks will need to be well washed to get any earth out. Turn the vegetables in the melting butter and add the oatmeal—the coarsest you can find. Add stock and salt and pepper. Simmer for 30–40 minutes. Dilute with water if too thick. Add the milk, adjust the seasoning, and reheat. Stir in the parsley or sprinkle it on top.

If you don't have all the suggested vegetables, carrot, onion and one other will still make a tasty soup.

Mushroom Soup

This is best made with big coarse Horse Mushrooms; we find those that grow in the heather have the most aromatic flavour. Failing these, cultivated mushrooms will do, but they should be the dark open kind, not buttons. If they are looking a bit past it, all the better for this soup, as it should be slightly pungent. There is no need to chop the mushrooms if you are going to liquidise it, but if not, break up the caps and chop the stalks. The soup should have chunks of mushroom and onion: it is not a purée.

½–¾ lb (225–350 g) mushrooms
1½ oz (40 g) butter
1 medium onion
1½ oz (40 g) flour (plain or
    wholemeal)
1-inch (2.5 cm) strip lemon rind
1 blade mace
1 small bay leaf
1 large pinch of thyme
1 pt (570 ml) light stock or water
salt and pepper
(cream *or* creamy milk *or* dry
    sherry—optional)

Chop the onion and turn in the butter with the mushrooms. Stir in the flour. Add everything else except the optional ingredients and stir to prevent sticking. Simmer, covered, for 20 minutes, but watch it at first as it tends to boil over.

Remove the bay leaf (if you can find it) and give the soup a short burst in the liquidiser. Reheat, add cream or sherry to taste, and adjust the seasoning.

Split Pea Soup with Cumin

This is an ordinary dull pea soup with a sprightly garnish. The result is lively and interesting, but you must serve it at once after adding the onion mixture, or the aroma will disappear.

For the soup:
¾ lb (350 g) onions, chopped
3 cloves of garlic, crushed
6 oz (175 g) yellow split peas
2 pt (1.2 l) water
salt

For the garnish:
1 oz (25 g) butter
1 medium onion finely sliced or chopped
½ a green pepper, chopped
1 tablespoon of chopped fresh mint
2 teaspoons of cumin seed
To finish:
yoghurt or cream

Put all the soup ingredients in a pan and cook till the peas are soft. If you soak them overnight first, this will only take about an hour —otherwise at least two hours. When the soup is ready, add more water if necessary and adjust the seasoning. Just before serving, fry all the garnish ingredients till the onion and pepper are softened but still slightly crisp. Splash this mixture into the hot soup and finish with a swirl of yoghurt or cream.

Potato Soup with Yoghurt

It is amazing how many spices curry haters will eat as long as you don't use the word "curry". This soup is, in fact, a very liquid curry, and if you want to make it hotter, a couple of chillies will do the trick.

¾ lb (350 g) onions, sliced fairly fine
2 oz (50 g) butter
2 teaspoons of fennel seeds
½ teaspoon of fenugreek seeds
½ teaspoon of mustard seeds
a large pinch of asafoetida
1 large bay leaf

2 cloves of garlic, crushed
1 teaspoon brown sugar
3 tomatoes, finely sliced
1 lb (450 g) potatoes, scrubbed and cubed
salt
1 pt (570 ml) water
¼ pt (150 ml) yoghurt

Grind the fennel, fenugreek and mustard. Fry the onions in the butter and when very hot add the ground spices, asafoetida and bay leaf. Stir for half a minute, then add the garlic and stir again. Add everything else except the yoghurt. Do not peel the potatoes or you will lose a lot of flavour, but if you can't stand tomato skin blanch the tomatoes first. Simmer the soup for about half an hour. If the potatoes are still intact, mash them a bit, but not too smooth. Adjust the salt, remove from the heat and stir in the yoghurt. Garnish with a pinch of paprika or chopped parsley.

Spinach Soup with Orange

This is my favourite soup and you will love it if you like spinach. If you don't like spinach much, you will find the orange disguises the taste quite pleasantly. If you detest spinach utterly, you will loathe a bowl of this stuff.

2 medium potatoes
2 medium onions
2 oz (50 g) butter
about 4 pints (2.4 l) of spinach
    leaves, pressed down firmly
2–3 inch (5–7.5 cm) strip orange
    rind
¼ pt (150 ml) water
juice of 1–2 oranges

Peel the onions and potatoes and cut them up roughly. Stew them in the butter while you wash the spinach. There is no need to remove the stems, but pick out seeding heads. Don't dry the spinach. Put it in on top of the other vegetables dripping wet and add the water and orange peel. Cook fairly fast till the spinach has shrunk and turned bright green, then simmer till the potato and onion are just cooked. Liquidise everything, adding more water if necessary. Add the orange juice and some salt, little by little, till the balance is right. Reheat without boiling. Garnish with a few shreds of freshly-pared orange rind. People won't eat them, but the colour contrast is pretty.

Two Chilled Soups

We don't usually have much need for cold soups in Harris. A hot afternoon may suggest pre-prandial drinks on the lawn, open windows, and a light cold supper, but by eight o'clock there is usually a forceful breeze and guests are donning woolly cardigans and looking hopefully at the unlit fire. However, there is occasionally a place for these two favourites. Borshcht is particularly useful, because if the weather deteriorates it can become a hot starter without altering the balance of the menu too much.

Borshcht

This recipe is a completely bogus adaptation of an assemblage of scholarly variants all claiming authenticity.

For the soup:
3 beetroots (about 1 lb (450 g) weight)
3 tomatoes
2 medium onions
1 medium carrot
3 stalks celery
1 oz (25 g) butter *or* 1 tablespoon oil*
1 teaspoon dill seeds or caraway seeds
1 pt (570 ml) water
salt and vinegar *or* lemon juice to taste*

For the garnish:
2 tablespoons sour cream (*or* 1 tablespoon cream & yoghurt)
a little salt
1 hard boiled egg
chopped parsley, dill or chives

*butter and lemon juice are better for a hot soup: oil and vinegar if to be served cold.

Twist off the leaves of the beetroots and put them in a pan of water *without skinning*. If you peel them all the juice and taste will bleed out. Boil till getting tender—about 15 minutes.

Skin the tomatoes and chop the flesh. Strain the seeds to save the juice. Chop all the other vegetables fairly finely and sauté in the butter for a couple of minutes. Add the tomato and its juice, dill or caraway, and salt.

Put the half-cooked beetroot into cold water and slip off the skins. Chop a third of the beetroot finely and add it and the whole beetroot to the soup. Simmer everything for about 15 minutes. Now fish out the whole beetroot, cut in chunks if large, and place in the liquidiser with a couple of ladles of the soup. Blend till smooth and return to the pan. Add the vinegar or lemon juice. (If you are serving the soup cold, cool and then chill it before seasoning to taste with vinegar and more salt if necessary). For the garnish, chop the hard-boiled egg and herbs separately. Salt the cream.

Hot or cold, this is a most colourful dish—bright crimson, marbled with the white of the cream and dusted with bright yellow and green from the egg and herbs.

Gazpacho

My Gazpacho is just as bogus as my Borshcht. The nearest I've been to España is at the bottom of a bottle of Xérès.

For the soup:
1 large cucumber *or* 2 small ones
1 red pepper
1 green pepper
4 tomatoes (about ¾ lb (350 g))
1 small onion
2 cloves garlic
1 tablespoon pine kernels *or* hazelnuts

1 tablespoon good olive oil
1 tablespoon wine vinegar
salt
2 sprigs of mint (about 10 leaves)
water
For the garnish:
cucumber, pepper, tomato and hard boiled egg, all chopped separately

Skin and seed the tomatoes. Strain and keep the juice from the seeds. Reserve the garnishes. You will need 1½ inches (3.75 cm) of the cucumber, a third of each pepper, a third of the tomato flesh, and one hard boiled egg.

Peel the rest of the cucumber, the onion and garlic. Cut these up enough to go in the liquidiser, with the oil, vinegar, tomatoes and juice. Add about ¼ pt (150 ml) water. As it liquefies, add all the other ingredients. If everything won't go in at once, it doesn't matter—you can stir it all together afterwards. You should end up with about two pints (1.2 l). Taste for seasoning—you may want more olive oil and vinegar than this.

Chill the soup while you chop the garnish finely. Arrange the chopped vegetables and egg in a delightful pattern on a pretty dish. Put a cube of ice in each bowl of soup and hand the garnishes separately.

The next two recipes are for **shellfish**. Velvet crabs, recognisable from their cobalt blue markings and pugnacious habits, often come up in lobster pots, so if you have ever put down your own pots, you have probably seen them. At the moment they are intensively fished for the European market, so they may not be with us long. Don't try to keep lobsters alive in a plastic bag or under a heap of seaweed: unless conditions are very cold, they will suffocate. You can keep them instead for up to 48 hours in a not too cold fridge (about 7°C/45°F). Wring out a towel in fairly salty cold water. Spread it out on the fridge shelf, lay the lobsters on it, and fold the towel over. When the door is closed, it will be dark, cool and quiet and the lobsters will lie doggo: they are used to spending a lot of time hiding in dark crevices. Do not leave lobsters out in the air or in a bright light, both of which are distressing for a secretive creature of the seabed.

Crabs are more difficult to keep, especially small ones: they should really be killed and used at once. For instructions on humane killing of shellfish, see the preamble to the "Shellfish" section on pp. 68–70. Don't buy dead crustaceans. They have almost certainly been boiled alive. Even for a single lobster in a large pot of fast boiling water death can take up to four minutes, but the method in common use is much more fiendish. Dozens of crustaceans are crammed together in wire baskets and placed in boiling vats, so that the heat takes God knows how long to kill off those in the middle. (The method is highly reminiscent of the twenty-foot high wickerwork giants stuffed with men and cats which the Druids annually sacrificed in a bonfire.)

I wouldn't recommend buying live crustaceans either, except on the quayside. They are often slow and moribund, having travelled for many hours, even days, packed in boxes, stressed, dehydrated and subjected to unfamiliar light, noise and movement. A proportion always die in transport. A healthy creature is snappy and lively when handled and doesn't blow bubbles.

You will notice I haven't mentioned the usual bogey of food poisoning. If you eat maltreated lobsters and crabs, I sincerely hope you get it, and badly.

Lobster Bisque

1 lobster of about 1 lb (450 g)
   weight
2 oz (50 g) butter
1 medium onion, finely chopped
2 teaspoons chopped tarragon
some parsley stalks
a 2-inch (5 cm) piece of lemon peel
1 oz (25 g) plain flour
1 pt (570 ml) water
1 glass white wine
salt, cayenne pepper, nutmeg
1 glass dry sherry
¼ pt (150 ml) cream

Kill the lobster by any of the recommended methods given on p. 69 and split it lengthwise. Keep the tail meat aside. Crack each joint of the large claws with a hammer and scrape the meat out with the handle of a teaspoon. Put this in a bowl, and add to it the greenish-yellow liver and the coral (if any). Pull out the stomach and digestive tract and discard. Pull out the body contents, scraping out any bits of meat you can get at, and (if the lobster was cooked) the curdy substance adhering to the inside of the shell. You are now left with a lot of small claws and bits of shell and a pool of juice. Crush all this somewhat with a hammer and put it in a sieve over a bowl to drain if it was very juicy.

Melt the butter and saute the onion in 1 oz (25 g) butter till golden. Add the drained lobster shells, turn the heat high, and fry the shell till some of its orange colour transfers to the butter. Add the tarragon, parsley stalks, lemon peel, water and wine. Boil this quite fiercely together for five minutes, and strain off and keep the resulting shellfish stock.

Put the stock in the liquidiser and add the contents of your bowl and the lobster juice if any. Blend well.

Melt the remaining butter, make a roux with the flour, and stir in the contents of the liquidiser. Simmer, stirring, for about three minutes—a bit longer if you started with a raw lobster. Season to taste.

Cut up the tail meat finely and add. If raw, simmer a further two minutes. If cooked, add the sherry and cream at once: after these go in, do not reboil. Adjust the seasoning—you may need a little lemon juice. Serve very hot, with a swirl of cream and a dusting of parsley or chervil on top.

37

Velvet Crab Soup

8 to 12 velvet crabs
water to cover the crabs
1 medium onion
2 cloves garlic, crushed
1 stick celery
2 oz (50 g) butter
1½ oz (40 g) flour
juice of half a lemon or a teaspoon
    of tomato purée

1 teaspoon French mustard
1 small bayleaf
1 blade mace
thyme and parsley
1 small glass very dry sherry or
    tannic red wine
cream or creamy milk to taste
salt

Stab the crabs and cook them for 10 minutes with just enough water to cover. Reserve the cooking liquid. If you have plenty of crabs, keep a few whole for people to crunch with their soup. For the rest, dismember them and make three heaps. (1) Twist off the large claws. (2) Press the line around the small claws on the underside till the body part comes free with these claws attached. (3) Remove the stomach sac and keep the body shells hollow side up to retain the juices and curd.

Now hammer the large claws to get out what meat you can. Put it in a bowl. Add any scraps you can pick from the underside portions, but don't bother to be too thorough. Scrape out the juices from the body shells but not the rest of the shells, which will still be meaty.

Melt the butter and chop the celery and onion finely. Sauté these gently with the garlic while you continue.

Put the shells you have left into the liquidiser, a few at a time, with a couple of ladles of the crab cooking liquid. Blend very thoroughly (this will sound dreadful). Strain the resulting mud through first one sieve and then another, adding more crab stock if necessary. When you have done this with all the shells, make up your strained liquid to 1¼ pints (700 ml) with crab stock.

Now stir the flour into the vegetable mixture and add the 1¼ pints (700 ml) of strained crab juices. Stir till it thickens. Add the crab meat in the bowl and all the other ingredients except the cream. Simmer for five minutes. Remove the bay leaf and mace, adjust the seasoning, and add as much cream or milk as you fancy. You may prefer more sherry. A good manzanilla is best.

I dish this soup in shallow plates with a crab swimming in each. Some people like to munch and suck the crabs. Others do not rejoice at the sight of their prey, but I don't see why they shouldn't be reminded of what they are eating.

Appetisers and Vegetarian Main Course Dishes

Except for the first few, most of the recipes in this section can also be used as vegetarian main dishes. The quantities given will serve six as a starter, or four as a main course in a full dinner menu. None of these recipes uses fish or meat. The sort of restaurant menu that sprouts game soups, pig terrines and shellfish mousses over the first two courses, followed by veal and poultry accompanied by lardon-bespattered salads and vegetables, gives me indigestion, physical and moral. I sometimes feel that the carnivorous would gladly complete the meal with sweetbreads in caramel or Stilton and pork crackling—are there ideas there for some ambitious young chef?

Light starters

First of all, a note on the terms "water ice", "granita", and "sorbet". Sorbet is a French concept. Fruit pulp is sweetened with sugar syrup and whipped egg white is added part way through freezing. To my mind, the result is too sweet, too bland, and too smooth for anything but a pudding. A granita has no egg white, the degree of sweetening is optional, and the texture is a sort of grainy slush. "Water ice" is a rather loose term. It used to be an English equivalent for both sorbet and granita. I would define it as a granita mixture which has been allowed to set rather firm. To their credit, and unlike sorbets, water ices and granitas can't be successfully kept. You must use them when they reach the correct texture, or they will become tasteless and lumpy.

Melon with Blackcurrant or Plum Water Ice

1 large ripe melon
For the ice:
1 lb (450 g) blackcurrants or santa
   rosa plums
light muscovado sugar to taste
water as required

Sieve the blackcurrants or plums. I liquidise them first, stones, stalks and all, and then press the pulp through a strainer using the back of a metal ladle. You should get about 1 pint (570 ml) of purée. Make it up with water if it is short. Sweeten to taste with muscovado sugar, a little at a time as it can easily get too sweet. The flavour should be fresh and intense. The ice will take about 1 to 1½ hours to freeze, during which you should mash it several times with a fork.

Cut off the very end pieces of the melon and divide it horizontally into six slices. Remove the seeds, and lay each slice on a flat plate. Put a scoop of the ice in the centre and decorate with attractive leaves or little sprigs of currants.

Redcurrants and Victoria plums also make good ices for serving with melon, but the colour contrast is not so attractive.

Grapefruit Water Ice

3 large or 5 small grapefruits
1 large orange
caster sugar to taste
¼ pt (150 ml) water

Using a very sharp knife, halve the grapefruits, cutting them zig-zag round their middles. Squeeze the grapefruit halves carefully, taking care not to damage the skins. Put the skins into a bowl of lukewarm water. Squeeze the orange, and strain and mix the two juices. You should have about 1¼ pints (700 ml)—if less, squeeze another grapefruit. Add the water, and sweeten to taste with caster sugar. Stir it vigorously to dissolve it before you decide to add more. Pour this mixture into a flat metal dish and freeze for about 1½–2 hours, mashing it well several times.

With a teaspoon, scrape the membrane and untidy bits out of the grapefruit skins. The soaking in water makes this easier. Dry the skins and freeze till the ice is ready. Serve the ice in the grapefruit cups.

For a party, these grapefruit ices look spectacular piled up on a silver or crystal dish full of cracked ice, bedecked with sprays of mint or other fresh greenery. The ice will keep them firm till people come to the table.

Avocado with Tomato Granita

3 avocadoes
a little lemon juice *or* French
    dressing
For the granita:
½ clove garlic
1 lb (450 g) tomatoes
1-inch (2.5 cm) strip orange rind
a sprig of marjoram or basil
a pinch of sugar
salt to taste
¼ pt (150 ml) water
To garnish:
6 nice sprigs of a compatible fresh
    herb—mint, basil or marjoram

Start the granita about two hours before you want to serve it. Put all the ingredients in the liquidiser, or chop finely. Sieve the mush, and test for seasoning. It should not be too salty, but not tasteless either. Pour into a flat-bottomed dish, preferably metal, and set on the floor of your freezing compartment. After ¾ hour, mash it with a fork, and repeat this as necessary to keep the mixture slushy and stop it sticking in a block to the bottom of the dish. If it does this at any stage, leave it at room temperature till it can be mashed again.

Slice the avocadoes lengthwise, just before serving, and taste a sliver. If they are dire, sprinkle liberally with French dressing: if they are so-so, brush with lemon juice: if they are superb, don't do anything to them. Serve a spoonful of tomato ice in the cavity, and garnish with the fresh herbs. (You can also use whole prawns as a garnish.)

Avocado and Walnut Salad

For the salad:
3 ripe avocadoes
2 large oranges
2 oz (50 g) shelled walnuts
For the dressing:
1 teaspoon chopped sweet cicely or
   mint
1 teaspoon honey
2 tablespoons yoghurt *or*
   1 tablespoon lemon juice and
   1 tablespoon sunflower oil
a pinch of salt
For the garnish:
lettuce leaves

Cut the avocado flesh into chunks and place in a deep bowl. Scatter on the walnut pieces. Obviously fresh newly shelled nuts are best, but others will do up to the very rim of rancidity.

Now place a strainer over the bowl. Using a very sharp knife, peel the oranges, round and round as you would apples, removing all the pith. Do this over the strainer so as not to lose any of the juice. With a fine saw-edged knife, cut out the orange segments, leaving all the membrane behind. Squeeze the remains of the orange hard in your fist over the strainer to get out the last of the juice. Mix the orange segments carefully with the avocado.

For the dressing:

Mix all the ingredients together. Sweet cicely is a common country wild flower, with a delicate aniseed flavour, but if you don't have it, mint will do. If your walnuts were grotty, use the oil dressing rather than yoghurt, but don't be tempted to use walnut oil for this salad—it is much too heavy.

Pour the dressing over the salad and mix, but gently. Chill, but not for more than half an hour. Dish surrounded by the lettuce and garnished with sprigs of the herb you used.

Melon with Mint and Yoghurt Dressing

3 ogen melons *or* 1 large honeydew
   melon
For the dressing:
¼ pt (150 ml) yoghurt
1 dessertspoon of honey, preferably
   heather
2 teaspoons lemon or orange juice
1 tablespoon finely chopped mint
For the garnish:
sprigs of mint

Chill the melons. Mix all the ingredients for the dressing: don't use an insipid honey. Lemon juice is best for ogens and orange for honeydew.

If using ogens, cut through the middle, remove the seeds and pour the dressing into the cavities. If using honeydew, get the flesh out with a melon-baller or cut into chunks. Divide between six glass dishes and pour the dressing over. Garnish with the sprigs of mint.

Vegetable Soufflés

The basic method for all hot soufflés is the same: you add egg yolks and the flavouring agent, puréed or chopped, and then fold in the stiffly whisked egg whites. A 3½-egg mixture will give you at least 8 individual soufflés. There are a few slight variations on the method, so I shall give separate hints for my favourite versions, after the basic instructions.

Soufflés are not entirely predictable. You may follow all the directions carefully and still end up with total collapse or failure to rise. However, the soufflés will still taste good—don't be too sensitive about such events. There are a few general hints here which will help to eliminate mistakes.

(1) Don't incorporate hidden water—it will affect the rising power of the egg whites, so:

Make sure all utensils are dry and at room temperature, to avoid condensation.

Don't work in a steamy kitchen or leave the separated egg whites in a damp atmosphere.

Drain your vegetables well, and if the purée is rather thin make the white sauce correspondingly thicker.

(2) Use only very fresh eggs. Don't leave the whisked egg whites standing—incorporate them immediately.

(3) Don't have too much top heat, which will form a hard crust and prevent the bottom from rising properly. Place your soufflés mid-way down the oven or a little lower. If you are really pernickity, place the filled soufflé dishes on a pre-heated baking sheet to get the rising started from the bottom first.

(4) Don't admit draughts or jolts. Open and close the oven very carefully, and when you are carrying the finished soufflés to the table, shut the windows. A sudden gust will shrivel them up. I have had several sad experiences when the dog has been deciding whether to go in or out or half-way through the back door at this unpropitious moment.

Basic Method

> 1½ oz (40 g) butter
> 1 oz (25 g) flour
> ¼ pt (150 ml) milk
> 4 eggs separated, or 3 yolks and
>   4 whites
> ½–¾ pt (275–425 ml) cooked
>   vegetables chopped very finely or
>   puréed
> seasoning

Pre-heat the oven to 200°C/400°F.

Butter 8 to 10 small ramekins or soufflé dishes lightly—not too much buttering or the rising mixture will slip back down the dish. Melt the butter, stir in the flour, and cook till it turns pale. Stir in the milk and boil, beating till you have a smooth thick sauce. Turn this into a wide bowl. Put a piece of wet greaseproof paper over it if the vegetable purée isn't ready, or a skin will form.

Beat in the vegetable purée and when it has cooled slightly, the egg yolks. Season to taste, quite highly—the egg whites will blunt the flavour somewhat.

Whisk the egg whites very stiff, and fold a third into the vegetable mixture, followed by the other two thirds. Use a rubber spatula or a metal spoon, with a light semi-circular slicing movement. Turn the mixture gently into the prepared dishes (filling within ¼ inch (6 mm) of the top is safe but not completely full or your soufflé will escape).

Bake the soufflés immediately for 35 minutes. Don't open the oven door till at least 30 have elapsed. If they look cooked then, experiment by pushing one dish slightly with your finger. If the contents quake, they're not quite ready.

For Cauliflower soufflés

Use one small head of cauliflower. Cut into small sprigs and cook in minimal water till tender. Purée with a little of the cooking water or milk and use less than ¼ pt (150 ml) of milk, for the white sauce. Beat in the purée while the sauce is hot. Sprinkling the tops of these soufflés with grated cheese is a wise precaution, as the cauliflower mixture tends to lack stamina and may collapse.

For Fennel soufflés

Use 1 lb (450 g) of fennel. Keep the nice bits of green and chop them finely. Trim and slice the heads and simmer in a little water with a knob of butter and a squeeze of lemon juice. Mash very well or purée, with its liquid, of which there should be very little. Fold this into the sauce with the chopped green leaves and 1 tablespoon of Pernod.

For Sweet Pepper soufflés

Slice 2 large red peppers and ½ a medium onion. Cook gently in 2 teaspoons oil till very soft. Rub through a sieve with the back of a ladle. Don't add extra liquid to this purée: this type of soufflé tends to sink anyway, but it is worth making for its brilliant colour and fresh summery taste.

For Spinach soufflés

Wash 1½ lb (675 g) of spinach. Put in a pan without added water. Cook till the leaves have wilted and the juices have run. Drain very well, chop finely, and add to the sauce. If you prefer, liquidise the spinach with some of the cooking liquid, and use less than ¼ pt (150 ml) milk for the sauce, but be sure to beat the purée into the sauce while it is hot or it will be very stiff to work. Season with nutmeg and freshly ground pepper.

While on the subject of soufflés, here is a related recipe.

Spinach Soufflé Flan

You could of course use any soufflé mixture to fill a pastry case, but this filling is less rich, though more collapsible.

For the pastry:
6 oz (175 g) wholewheat flour
5 tablespoons sunflower oil
2 oz (50 g) strong grated cheese
water to mix

For the filling:
1 lb (450 g) fresh spinach *or*
  1 × 12 oz (340 g) tin
½ oz (15 g) butter
½ oz (15 g) flour
salt
nutmeg or coriander
2 eggs
(1 tablespoon grated
  cheese—optional)

Preheat the oven to 200°C/400°F.
For the pastry:

Mix all the ingredients, using just enough water to make a firm dough. Roll out carefully. It will break up, but press it bit by bit into an 8-inch (20 cm) flan ring placed on a baking sheet. Bake blind till just firm, about 20 minutes. Remove from the oven, cool slightly, and carefully lift off the flan ring. If the pastry starts breaking, leave the ring on—it will look inelegant, but at least the filling won't escape.

For the filling:

If using fresh spinach, wash well, shake off excess water, and cook till wilted. Drain well, reserving the liquid, and chop the leaves. For tinned spinach, drain and keep the juice.

Make a roux with the butter and flour. When it turns pale, add spinach juice cautiously to make a very thick sauce. Put this in a wide bowl with the chopped spinach and beaten egg yolks. Mix well and season.

Whisk the egg whites very stiff and fold lightly into the spinach mixture. Turn this gently into the prepared flan case (it can mound up in the middle, but if it slops over the edges, take a bit out and cook it separately in a greased dish).

Scatter the grated cheese on top, and return to the oven for about 30 minutes. Look in cautiously and touch the centre at that point—if it is liquid underneath give it another five minutes.

Stuffed Vegetables

Stuffed vegetables are delicious either as a starter or a main course but they do tend to look awful. Their original bright colours are subdued to dingy shades of khaki and brown; they exude puddles of watery juice on the plate; they break up on serving and disembowel themselves slowly on the diners' plates or in extreme cases into their laps. There isn't really all that much to be done about this: a smothering of chopped parsley is the best policy, but I often don't have any because our heavy dog sunbathes in the parsley patch.

If you are serving these dishes as a main course, a sauce made with the juices and a roux of flour and butter will improve the appearance and make more of a meal. Make your sauce, taste, and season with what you fancy—white wine, lemon juice, tomato purée, grated cheese, etc. Don't let the flavouring overpower the stuffing, though. I don't advise over-enthusiastic applications of Worcester sauce, curry powder or French mustard, for example.

Apple-stuffed Mushrooms

If possible, choose large mushrooms 2 inches (5 cm) or more in diameter for this dish. You will need about 12 of that size for this quantity of stuffing. You can use smaller ones but they are more fiddly to deal with.

15 large mushrooms *or*	2 large tart eating apples
¾ lb (350 g) small ones	salt and freshly ground pepper
1 medium onion	thyme, marjoram and parsley to taste
4 oz (100 g) butter	½ glass white wine

Take the stems out of the mushrooms and chop them finely with three of the large caps or 2 oz (50 g) of the smaller mushrooms. Lay the whole caps close together in one layer in an ovenproof dish.

Chop the onion fairly finely and cook it gently till it softens in 3 oz (75 g) of the butter.

Grate the apples, skin and all, and add to the onion along with the chopped mushrooms. Add seasoning and herbs to taste.

Divide this mixture between the mushroom caps, pressing it down with a finger. Melt the rest of the butter and dribble this over the mushrooms. Pour the white wine into the dish.

Bake the mushrooms, uncovered, in a moderate oven for 15 minutes. When you dish them, spoon over any juice: the mushrooms will re-absorb it.

Stuffed Peppers

A very similar stuffing to the last one makes an unusual and unstodgy complement to peppers. The most attractive effect is achieved by using peppers of different colours, red, green, and yellow.

    1 tablespoon olive oil
    6 smallish peppers
    1 medium onion
    3 oz (75 g) butter
    6 oz (175 g) mushrooms
    2 tart eating apples
    1 tablespoon almond kernels
    salt and ground black pepper
    thyme and parsley
    lemon juice

Put the olive oil in a casserole in which the peppers can sit upright close together. Cut off the tops of the peppers, but keep them. Discard the seeds. Trim the bases if they are too knobbly to stand, but try not to make holes. Put the peppers in the casserole.

Chop the onions and fry in the butter till golden. Chop the mushrooms, grate the apples, skin and all, and chop the almonds coarsely: blanch them or not, as you please. Add all these ingredients to the onions. Season to taste. If the mixture is too sweet, add lemon juice, but you may not need it.

Fill this stuffing into the peppers. Replace the tops and put about two tablespoons of water in the casserole. Cover with a lid or foil and bake in a moderate oven for about 40 minutes. Check once or twice to make sure there is still a little liquid in the base of the dish.

These peppers are best accompanied by a sauce. I make about half a pint (275 ml) of thick white sauce and add 2 oz (50 g) grated cheese and the pan juices. If there isn't much juice, make a thinner sauce and add a good squeeze of lemon or a tablespoon of dry vermouth.

Sesame-stuffed Aubergines

Not everyone likes aubergines. Perhaps it is their funereal colour. When dealing with them, there are three points to remember.

(1) If not salted and drained first they can be bitter, and are indefinably unpleasant in texture.

(2) They will drink as much oil as you give them at once—gallons of it—and then you will get indigestion: so add it bit by bit, as sparingly as possible.

(3) Undercooked aubergines are repulsive.

Properly treated, they are superb, particularly in spicy dishes. This one was invented to use up a large bag of sesame seeds, but the combination is so good I now use it often—see another example in the section on cereals and vegetable side dishes (p. 97).

3 medium aubergines
1 tablespoon coriander seeds
1 teaspoon black peppercorns
2 teaspoons paprika
a large pinch of asafoetida
2 oz (50 g) butter
2 tablespoons unhulled sesame
    seeds

¼ pt (150 ml) yoghurt
2 medium onions, roughly chopped
1 clove garlic
a few sprigs of mint
juice of half a lemon

Slice the aubergines in half lengthwise. Scoop out the flesh, leaving the skin intact. Chop the flesh roughly. Salt the chopped aubergine and put it in a colander. Salt the skin cases on the inside, and turn them hollow side down on top of the contents of the colander. Allow the whole lot to drain for 45 minutes, then wash it in cold water and pat it dry in a tea-towel.

Grind the coriander and pepper and set aside.

Put the yoghurt, lemon juice, onions, garlic and mint in a liquidiser and reduce to a paste. If you haven't a liquidiser, grate the onion and chop the mint finely, crush the garlic, and mix these into the yoghurt with the lemon juice.

Get the butter very hot. Fry the coriander, pepper, paprika and asafoetida for half a minute. Add the sesame seed and the chopped aubergine and stir well. Pour in the yoghurt mixture. Lower the heat and cook gently, uncovered, till the aubergine is fairly soft—about 10 minutes. Arrange the scooped-out aubergine shells in a shallow oven-proof dish, keeping them close together to support each other. Fill with the cooked mixture. Sprinkle with sesame oil or dot with butter, and bake for about 40 minutes in a moderately hot oven. If they look like drying up, reduce the heat and pour a tablespoon or so of water into the dish.

Spicy Stuffed Tomatoes

The stuffing is really just a very thick dahl. For the spices, consult any recipe for garam masala, or make up your own, but don't use ready ground spices.

Suggested combinations: coriander, cumin, cinnamon, cloves.
coriander, cumin, cardamoms, bay leaf.
coriander, kalonji, cinnamon, asafoetida.

Add a fresh chilli to the lentils if you want it to be hot.

    6 large tomatoes
    1-inch (2.5 cm) piece of tamarind
        pulp *or* juice of 1 lemon
    2 oz (50 g) red lentils
    1 small onion
    2 cloves garlic
    1 oz (25 g) butter
    1 dessertspoon of freshly ground
        spices
    1 tablespoon chopped parsley or
        mint
    salt

Cut lids off the tomatoes and scoop out the seeds. Set them close together in a greased ovenproof dish or 6 ramekins. Soak the tamarind in half a cup of hot water and strain this through a sieve, or squeeze the lemon. Simmer the lentils for ¾ hour with twice their volume of water and the tamarind or lemon juice. Check now and again to forestall sticking.

Grate the onion and crush the garlic. Fry in the butter till browning. Add the spices and fry for one more minute.

When the lentils are soft and have absorbed the water, mix them with the spices and onions and the fresh herbs. Salt to taste. Stuff the tomatoes with this mixture and bake uncovered in a moderate oven for 10 to 15 minutes.

Other Vegetable Appetisers

I have chosen these because they are attractive to look at—important for a first course—and also easy to prepare. Except for the mushroom dish, they don't need last minute attention, but don't keep them standing once cooked: most cooked vegetables weep and you will find them looking distinctly depressed if they are kept warm for more than five minutes.

Aubergine Pizza

For the base:
2 large aubergines (about 1½ lb)
   (675 g)
For the topping:
3 tablespoons olive oil
1 medium onion
3 cloves garlic
2 lb (900 g) tomatoes
1 teaspoon dried oregano or basil,
   or a mixture
3 oz (75 g) grated cheddar or other
   tasty cheese
salt
10 black olives

Slice the aubergines into rings a bit less than ½-inch (1.25 cm) thick. Put the slices in a colander, salt them liberally and leave to drain for 45 minutes.

Chop the onion and garlic fairly fine. Fry gently in the hot oil till they soften slightly. Add the tomatoes cut in half and the herbs. Simmer till the onion is very soft—about 20 minutes. If the mixture looks watery, raise the heat and boil till it thickens.

Press this mixture through a sieve if you want a dressier dish. Add 2 oz (50 g) of the cheese and salt to taste. Now turn the aubergines into a basin of cold water to rinse off the salt. Dry them thoroughly in a tea-towel. Oil a pizza plate very well. (If you don't have one, any large shallow ovenproof dish will do: my favourite is a huge cast iron gratin dish.) Lay the aubergines all over the bottom, close together or overlapping. Pour the topping on and scatter the remaining cheese over and decorate with the olives. Bake in a moderately hot oven for 20–30 minutes. To test for readiness, poke a knife into the centre: if there is no resistance, the aubergine is cooked.

Courgettes with Cheese

It goes without saying that this is best made with very young fresh courgettes. It can also be adapted as an accompanying vegetable dish—in which case use 1 lb (450 g) of courgettes and ¾ pt (425 ml) milk and omit the cream.

½ lb (225 g) courgettes	¼ pt (150 ml) cream
1 small onion	½ pt (275 ml) milk
½ oz (15 g) butter	salt, pepper and nutmeg
1 whole egg + 2 yolks	3 oz (75 g) grated cheese.

Slice the courgettes thinly—about ¼ inch (6 mm) thick. Drop the slices into a pan of boiling water and simmer till just tender. This will take from one to three minutes depending on the age of the courgettes. Drain them well.

Chop the onion finely and fry till soft in the butter.

Butter 6 small ramekins or a two-pint (1.2 litre) ovenproof dish. Put the onion in at the bottom and the courgettes on top.

Beat the remaining ingredients together and pour over the courgettes. Stir while you are doing this or the cheese will be unevenly distributed.

Bake in a moderately hot oven till just set and brown on top—about 15 minutes for the small dishes and 25 minutes for the large.

Carrot Cake

This is bastard oriental. It looks very attractive and tastes a lot better than the list of ingredients might lead you to expect.

2 large carrots (about ¾ lb)
20 cardamoms
2 teaspoons oil—sesame oil is best
    with carrots
salt
1 tablespoon raisins
1 large leek

Grate the carrot and fry in the oil. Add the black seeds scraped out of the cardamoms—discard the husks. When the carrot is golden add a tablespoon of water and continue cooking while this evaporates. Add salt.

Butter a 7-inch (17.5 cm) sandwich tin, preferably non-stick. Scatter the raisins on the bottom, then the carrot mixture. Cut the leek into narrow rings, wash to remove grit, drain, and press the leek down on top of the carrot. Cover with a greased paper. Bakewell rounds are great for the purpose.

Cook for 15 minutes in a moderately hot oven. Remove from the oven, press down on the paper, and allow the tin to stand for 5 minutes. Remove the paper, run a knife round the edge of the tin, and turn out on a plate.

Curd Cheese Ramekins

Here's the humble carrot again, but you will find it difficult to detect. The curd cheese is made with drained yoghurt—for details see p. 153.

For the base:
6 oz (175 g) curd cheese
3 oz (75 g) wholemeal
  breadcrumbs
3 oz (75 g) cheddar cheese, grated
1 medium carrot
1 small onion
2 oz (50 g) mushrooms
1 tablespoon parsley
1 tablespoon double cream
1 egg
milk to mix
salt and pepper

For the sauce:
½ pt (275 ml) milk
1 small onion
1 teaspoon dried thyme
1 oz (25 g) butter
1 oz (25 g) flour
salt

For the base:
Grate the carrot and chop the onion, mushrooms and parsley. Mix all the ingredients together, but reserve 1 oz (25 g) each of the breadcrumbs and grated cheese. Use only enough milk to produce a thick paste. Butter 6 small ramekins or a two-pint (1.2 litre) ovenproof dish, and spread the curd mixture in the bottom.
For the sauce:
Heat the milk gently for 15 minutes, with the sliced onion and thyme. Strain the milk and use it to make a white sauce with the remaining ingredients. Pour this over the curd mixture and sprinkle on the rest of the crumbs and cheese. Make sure the dishes have at least ½ inch (1.25 cm) spare room at the top or they will bubble over. Bake in a moderate oven for 25–30 minutes.

Gougère of Mushrooms and Peppers

A classic gougère is made with a choux paste incorporating small chunks of gruyère cheese. As I can't get gruyère cheese and don't like it anyway, I use grated cheddar. We get majestic aged whole farmhouse cheeses weighing a portly half hundredweight, of a character and substance far exceeding any flighty continental, so I use cheddar for practically every cheesey purpose. Indeed, I would be afraid to use anything else, with one of these enthroned on its trestle eyeing me sternly from the pantry. I need hardly say that there is no point at all in using grated orange plastic from the supermarket.

Gougère is quite a dressy dish, well worth mastering. You can vary it by omitting the cheese or using different fillings, but whatever you put in the middle should be piquantly seasoned and not too watery. Certain vegetables are worth avoiding in this context. Gougère of cabbage and turnip?

For the pastry:
3¾ oz (100 g) plain flour
3 oz (80 g) butter
7½ fl oz (200 ml) water
3 well beaten eggs
1½ oz (40 g) grated cheese

For the filling:
1 tablespoon oil
1 medium onion
1 clove garlic
2 medium red peppers
2 teaspoons tomato purée
2 teaspoons fresh chopped
    marjoram, *or* ½ teaspoon dried
2 teaspoons fresh chopped parsley
½ lb (225 g) mushrooms
salt and a pinch of sugar

Preheat the oven to 190°C/375°F.
For the pastry:
    Sift the flour on to a sheet of paper.
    Cut the butter into chunks and place in a wide pan with the water, over a medium heat. When the butter melts, turn up the heat so that the mixture boils up. Remove from the heat immediately and tip in the flour all at once. Beat hard till the mixture leaves the sides of the pan. Beat in the eggs bit by bit—if they are large, you will probably need only about 2½. The paste should be soft, but hold its shape. Lastly beat in the grated cheese.
    Grease an 8-inch (20 cm) diameter baking dish and arrange the paste in spoonfuls evenly round the edge. It puffs up enormously so don't be alarmed at how meagre it looks. Place in the middle of the oven and when the pastry has puffed up but not darkened (about 25 minutes)

raise the heat to 205°C/400°F and give it a further 10 minutes. It should be light, crisp and golden brown.

For the filling:

Chop up the onion finely and sauté in the hot oil till tender. Add the pepper, finely sliced, and the crushed garlic. Turn these in the oil, cover, and cook on a very low heat for 10 minutes. Slice the mushrooms, stalks and all. Put them with all the remaining ingredients in the pan and mix well. If no juice formed round the stewing pepper and onion, you will need to add two tablespoons of water. Cover the pan again and remove from the heat: the mushrooms and herbs should not be overcooked.

When the gougère is ready to come out of the oven, heat up the filling quickly on a high heat, take out the gougère, and pour the filling into the hole in the centre. Serve at once if possible, but you can return it to the turned-off oven for 5 minutes if necessary.

Pepper Fritters with Tomato Granita

Tomato ice is a delicious surprise with hot vegetable fritters. The combination is agonising for those with sensitive teeth.

> 1 quantity tomato granita *(see recipe for Avocado with tomato granita on p. 41)*
> 1 red and 1 green pepper
> 4 oz (100 g) plain flour
> 1 egg, separated
> ¼ pt (150 ml) milk
> ½ teaspoon salt
> fat for deep frying

Sift the flour and salt, and mix in the egg yolk and milk till smooth. Beat well and set aside. Slice the peppers into long strips not more than ½ inch (1.25 cm) wide. Heat the fat to the correct temperature—about 205°C/400°F.

Whisk the egg white stiffly and fold into the fritter batter, then put the pepper strips into the bowl. Fry them in batches till golden and drain on kitchen paper. While they are cooking, dish a scoop of the granita on to cold plates. Arrange the fritters round the granita and serve at once, before they go cold or soggy.

Devilled Mushrooms

I call these "devilled mushrooms" for want of a better name, but the dish is not exceptionally spicy. The main flavouring is actually mint. I have an embarrassment of this herb. It is one of the few that grow enthusiastically here, and I feel obliged to use it frequently. It is extremely good with mushrooms. Mushroom Humbug, perhaps.

For the mushrooms:
2 oz (50 g) butter
1 small onion
¾ lb (350 g) mushrooms
2 cloves garlic
1-inch (2.5 cm) piece of fresh
    ginger (optional)
1 tablespoon chopped mint
1 teaspoon brown sugar
juice of half a lemon
salt, black pepper and nutmeg
1–2 teaspoons flour
3 tablespoons cream

For the topping:
1 oz (25 g) butter
1 clove garlic
2 tablespoons brown breadcrumbs
chilli powder or cayenne pepper

Chop the onion finely and sauté in the butter. Chop the mushroom stems and a few of the caps, crush the garlic, and grate the ginger. When the onion is tender, add all these ingredients and fry together over a medium heat for two minutes.

Add the mint, sugar, lemon juice and other seasonings, and stir till the lemon juice is absorbed. Sprinkle in the flour and cook a further minute—you may need a little more butter.

Add the cream, and let the mixture just bubble. Remove from the heat. You can do this much up to half an hour ahead.

Now prepare the topping. Crush the garlic and fry it with the breadcrumbs and butter till crisp. Add chilli cautiously to the strength you like. You can do this ahead, too.

To serve, stir the reserved mushroom caps into the mushroom sauce and reheat quickly, but without boiling. Dish into individual hot bowls or plates and sprinkle on the spiced breadcrumbs.

Fish

We are lucky in being able to obtain a reasonable variety of fresh fish locally, though usually only two or three types are available in any one week. Where possible I favour large energetic fish, as they are usually clouted on the head when hauled inboard to stop them wreaking havoc with the gear, and so suffer a less miserable end than the smaller creatures left to flap and suffocate.

Most popular with guests is salmon. Islanders, on the whole, think little of it, after the first few summer meals. They cram their freezers with it, to assuage the longings of visiting winter relatives. They feed it to dogs and hens and stuff it into sandwiches for their bed-and-breakfast visitors' late night snack. In the old days they used to salt it, and nowadays some people have some smoked at MacDonald's excellent smokehouse in Stornoway (no relation of the hamburgers).

While the populace at large are turning green at the sight of salmon, the Barbour-bedecked and fly-festooned rod fishermen eagerly flog loch and river for the first bite of the season. Their fish may cost them £500 a whack. They must be crazy. Also cruel: would they like to spend their last half hour being dragged along by a hook through the cheek or nostril? I prefer salmon to be netted, as they then drown quite quickly. Monofilament nets are atrocious, though, as they maim and kill not only their intended catch, but also otters, seals, and seabirds in vast numbers.

The next three recipes are for **halibut**. I think this is the best of all fish, firm-fleshed and clean-tasting. If, like me, you get your fish whole and are then faced with gutting, filleting and skinning, it is the easiest of all to deal with. It is not slimy, or oily. Its skin doesn't tear, its guts don't stink, and its bones don't jab you. There is very little wasted of the body weight, and the pressure-cooked head makes a delicious breakfast for hens. It is an inoffensive creature in life and death, a peaceful bottom-feeder relying on camouflage to induce the world to pass it by. Unlike the sad-faced whiting, it does not conceal a gutleful of its smaller fellows. In recent years my respectful affection for the halibut has come in the way of my taste for its flesh, but I can still vouch for the excellence of these three recipes.

Halibut with Mushrooms

This is delicious with new potatoes. It is good cold as the basis for a salad, too. If the cream you are going to use is fresh and unadulterated and the halibut likewise, you will not need flour in the sauce, as it will set to a delicious curd anyway. Our cream rarely lives up to our fish, so I usually add the flour, reluctantly. It tastes better without. Do not overcook this dish—halibut is not at all disgusting even a bit on the raw side.

1½–2 lb (675–900 g) piece of halibut on the bone	1 teaspoon flour (optional)
6 oz (175 g) mushrooms	2 teaspoons tomato purée
1 small onion	4 tablespoons double cream
1 oz (25 g) butter	salt and pepper
½ teaspoon each dried thyme and tarragon	

Cut the fish into steaks about ¾-inch (2 cm) thick, or skin and fillet it and cut into even-sized portions.

Chop the onion finely and sauté in the butter till transparent. Chop the mushroom stalks finely, break the caps into three or four pieces, and stir into the onion mixture till the fat is absorbed.

Add the flour if you are going to use it and then all the remaining ingredients. Spread half this mixture on the bottom of an ovenproof dish of a size to take the fish in a single close-packed layer. Spread the rest of the mushroom mix on top of the fish and bake in a moderate oven for 15–20 minutes.

Halibut in Tomato Cream

1½–2 lb (675–900 g) piece of
  halibut
1½ lb (675 g) ripe tomatoes
1 small onion
½ teaspoon dried tarragon or basil
1-inch (2.5 cm) strip orange or
  lemon peel

¼ pt (150 ml) double cream
salt
chopped parsley or slices of raw
  tomato for garnish

Cut up the fish as for the preceding recipe. This dish looks more attractive if the dark skin at least is removed.

Chop the onion finely and cut the tomatoes in half. Put these ingredients in a wide pan with the herbs and peel. Prod this about over a high heat till the juice runs from the tomatoes, then lower to a simmer and cook for 10 minutes. If is sticks, add a little water—don't let it darken, which tomatoes do if they dry out.

Press this mixture through a sieve. Add the cream, and salt to taste. Lay the pieces of fish in a shallow dish and pour the sauce over. Bake uncovered in a very moderate oven for 20–25 minutes. Don't let the edges brown: the sauce should keep its clear colour. Decorate with chopped parsley or the tomato slices.

Halibut with Herbs and Lemon

This is a very easy and delicious way of baking any sort of white fish.

1½–2 lb (675–900 g) piece of
  halibut
juice of 1 lemon and grated rind of
  ½ lemon
¼ pt (150 ml) double cream +
  2 tablespoons top of the milk

salt
1 tablespoon chopped parsley
1 tablespoon snipped chives
1 tablespoon any other mixed fresh
  herbs—dill, chervil, thyme,
  tarragon

Cut up the fish as in the preceding recipes. Mix all the ingredients for the sauce together and pour over the fish. Bake uncovered in a very moderate oven for 20–25 minutes. The sauce will probably curdle even at a low heat but it is still very good.

Turbot with Dill Sauce

Turbot is highly esteemed by most discriminating persons including our dog, but I don't like dealing with it. In its whole state it is too rhomboidal for any vessel but a turbotière, an extravagant and unstoreable piece of equipment. If you cut it up, it blunts your knives, breaks your scissors, and smears you with irritant and irremovable slime. It wears pathetic knobbly camouflage on its dark side, and its face is understandably one of failure and sadness. But for all that it is a delicacy, with its rich creamy flesh, so I give one recipe here.

2 lb (900 g) turbot fillet
For the sauce:
4 egg yolks
1 teaspoon vinegar
8 oz (225 g) unsalted butter
juice of half an orange
finely grated rind of 1 orange

6 green olives
1 teaspoon capers
2 tablespoons dill
2 teaspoons snipped chives
For the garnish:
1 orange

Fillet the turbot and cut into serving pieces. Leave the skin on, and lay skin down on a buttered trivet or baking dish. Steam, or bake in a moderate oven covered with buttered greaseproof paper. It will only take about 10 minutes. It remains very firm but turns opaque when cooked.

For the sauce:

Start as for a hollandaise sauce. Put the egg yolks in a bowl or double boiler with the vinegar and a small lump of the butter, which should be very soft. Set the bowl over (*not* in) a pan of steaming water and stir constantly while you add the rest of the butter bit by bit. If you are lazy and reckless, put the butter in by halves. Beat away at the first half till it has melted, then do the same with the other half. By then it should be thick and lukewarm, no hotter or it will curdle.

Chop the olives, capers and dill, snip the chives, grate the orange rind and squeeze the juice. Add all these to the sauce and taste for salt. Keep the sauce just warm—no more.

For the garnish:

Slice the orange into very thin slices through the middle.

Dish the turbot, pour the sauce over, decorate with the orange slices and serve at once.

Mackerel are the subject of the next two recipes.

People suspect that mackerel are cheap, if not free. It is therefore impossible to serve them to our hotel guests without causing sulks. This is a pity, because fresh mackerel is unbeatable. They are oily so should be spiked with some sharply aromatic flavour. The following method made a virtue of necessity when a friend and I were barbecuing freshly caught fish on a remote beach. Investigating the hillside for thyme or juniper, we found none, but smelt bog-myrtle. We suspected it might be poisonous, but stuffed the bellies of the fish with it anyway. It was delicious. Bog-myrtle won't grow in your garden, but it can be gathered and dried like bay.

Kill the mackerel as soon as you take them off the hook. It is in your interest as well as theirs. Comparisons in our fish-catching days showed that our fish (instantly despatched) always tasted better than friends' fish caught at the same time and left to suffocate. The latter had an indescribable off-taste, slightly metallic, not quite clean, even in a very fresh fish. Presumably the chemicals produced by stress cause the change. It is well known that the production of adrenalin in warm-blooded animals just before slaughter affects the quality of the meat. Depraved tastes prefer this tortured flesh: Rouennais ducklings are smothered and dogs in the Philippines and South Korea are slowly strangled to lend a fiendish goût to the meat.

Grilled Mackerel

To more cheerful matters. Do thus with your cleanly killed mackerel.

    6 mackerel (about 12 oz (350 g)
        each)
    ½ oz (15 g) butter per fish
    3 sprigs bog-myrtle per fish (or use
        thyme instead)

Gut the fish and remove the heads. Make 3 diagonal slashes about ½ inch (1.25 cm) deep on each side. Put a flake of butter in each cut, and the remainder into the cavity with the bog-myrtle.

Grill at medium heat for about 7 minutes each side. If you are doubtful about doneness, poke a sharp knife between flesh and spine at the thickest part. If it doesn't come away easily, grill for a few minutes longer.

Pour the pan-juices over the fish and serve with lemon and mustard separately.

Smoked Mackerel Salad

This will serve six as a starter, or two to three as a lunch dish with a green salad. A sweetish brown bread is good with this.

For the salad:
2 large fillets of smoked mackerel
2 sticks celery
1 eating apple
½ small onion
For the dressing:
2 tablespoons mayonnaise *(for a recipe, see p. 72)*
2 teaspoons French mustard, preferably Dijon
3 tablespoons yoghurt
cayenne pepper and freshly ground black pepper
For the garnish:
parsley and lemon slices

To take the mackerel off the skin, hold the tail end under your left hand, and slice from the other end, slanting each cut to the right and twisting the blade flat as you reach the skin. Cut across into ½-inch (1.25 cm) slices. Slice the celery and apple thinly and chop the onion finely. Mix all these in a bowl.

For the dressing:
Combine all the ingredients in a separate bowl. If it is too bland, add lemon juice and more cayenne pepper. It should be quite sharp and tingling. Mix salad and dressing just before serving and decorate with parsley and lemon slices.

Haddock Mousse

This cold dish—rather solid for a mousse really—is suitable for a salad lunch or supper, or for a starter. If it is set in a fish-shaped mould, you can have great fun decorating it. Use strips of pimento for a sad fishy mouth, capers for eyes, and thin half slices of cucumber for scales, with a scattering of paprika on the back. Surround your masterpiece with lettuce leaves, tomato slices and fronds of dill. This is the best fun since making tri-coloured jelly at the age of five.

The recipe also works well with salmon, smoked salmon and smoked haddock.

For the mousse:
¾ lb (350 g) haddock fillet *or* 1½
   lb (675 g) whole fish
½ pt (275 ml) milk
½ bay leaf or a blade of mace
2 teaspoons gelatine + 2
   tablespoons water
1 oz (25 g) butter
1 oz (25 g) flour
any or all of the following:
   2 teaspoons lemon juice
   a dash of tabasco
   a tablespoon of finely chopped
     parsley
about half a small carton of double
   cream

For the garnish:
any salad things or fresh herbs
tomato-flavoured mayonnaise
   (optional)

Gut the fish if whole. Poach gently in the milk with the bay leaf and mace. It will take about 10–15 minutes, either in a very moderate oven or on the stove top. Cool slightly, remove all skin and bone, and crush the flesh. You can either chop it very finely, or put it briefly in a liquidiser with the minimum necessary of the cooking liquor.

Make a white sauce with the butter, flour and the remaining liquor from the fish. You may need a bit more or less milk—it shouldn't be runny, but should still fall from the spoon easily. Turn it into a wide bowl and add the chopped fish.

Soften the gelatine in the cold water and dissolve over gentle heat. If it boils it won't work properly.

Add the gelatine to the fish mixture together with the chosen flavourings, and salt to taste. Put aside to cool, stirring occasionally or it will set round the edges. If you are in a hurry, put the bowl in the freezer or in a basin of iced water. Whip the cream till it just holds its shape. When the mixture in the bowl is cold and setting, fold in the cream. Turn it into a dampened mould to set.

To serve, dip the mould very briefly (try 3 seconds) in very hot water. Loosen the mousse by pressing a finger over the top of it till it pulls away from the edges of the mould. Turn it on to a plate and decorate attractively. You can serve tomato mayonaise separately.

To make tomato mayonnaise, add two tablespoons of thin cream, two teaspoons of tomato purée and a few drops of tabasco to ¼ pint (150 ml) of bland mayonnaise (there is a recipe for mayonnaise on p. 72). This sauce does nothing at all for the smoked fish mousse or for salmon, but is good with haddock.

Turnover of Sole

This sounds like a lot of work, but it is actually not much trouble, as long as you have something else to keep you busy while the pastry is chilling, the stock brewing, and the sauce cooling.

If you had a fine Dover sole, you would not waste it on this dish, but it is a good way of using undistinguished flatfish such as lemon sole, megrims or witch. Years ago I used to use frozen puff pastry, and everyone thought it was a triumph. Now I always make my own and great lumps of it are left. Nevertheless, I continue to believe that even the roughest of homemade pastry is more wholesome than anything out of a shop freezer. If you like the taste of anti-oxidants and are addicted to glucose syrup, by all means use the packet stuff. Or try plasticine instead.

For the pastry:
9 oz (250 g) plain flour
a pinch of salt
5 oz (150 g) butter, straight from the fridge
ice-cold water
beaten egg to glaze

For the filling:
3–4 lb (1.4–1.8 kg) whole flatfish
     or 1¼ lb (550 g) fillets
1 bay leaf
1 small onion
1 small glass white wine
¼ pt (150 ml) milk, or more
1 oz (25 g) butter
1½ oz (40 g) flour
2 tablespoons cream
½ teaspoon dried tarragon *or*
     1 tablespoon chopped parsley
salt and pepper

For the pastry:

Mix the flour and salt in a wide bowl. Cut the butter into chunks (roughly ½-inch (1.25 cm) cubes) and drop into the flour. Add enough cold water to make a pliant dough, softer than shortcrust but not as soft as scones.

Knead out lightly into an oblong on a well-floured board. *Roll out to about ¼ inch (6 mm) thick, keeping everything well floured. Mark the oblong into thirds across its long dimension. Fold the right flap over the middle section and the left flap over that. Turn it so that the right-hand edge is facing you.*

Repeat the section between asterisks twice more. If your kitchen is hot, you may need to chill the pastry between operations, but this is only a distant and slovenly relation of puff pastry, so don't get too worked up about it. However, once the rolling is all finished, you are best to chill the pastry for at least half an hour.

For the filling:

If you start with whole fish, fillet them, and if you are fussy remove at least the dark skins. If you are leaving the skins on, do scale the fish before you start. Put all the trimmings in a wide pan with the onion, bay leaf, wine and ¼ pt (150 ml) of water. Leave the lid slightly off, and boil on a high heat for 5 minutes. Cover the pan, remove from the heat, and leave to sit till you are ready for it.

If you are using fillets, chop the onion, and infuse it with the bay leaf in the milk for 10 minutes over gentle heat, then strain.

Melt the butter, stir in the flour, and when it turns pale, add the milk. Beat till smooth. Add the strained fish liquor if you have it, or the wine if you started with fillets. If the sauce is still very thick, add more milk. Add the herbs and seasonings and simmer for 2 minutes. Fold in the cream and cool.

Cut the pastry in half and roll out into 2 oblongs about ⅛ inch (3 mm) thick. (One turnover would be too difficult to lift off the tray.) Place the sheets of pastry at opposite ends of a baking sheet, with one half of each piece hanging over the end of the tray. Brush the edges of the sections on the tray with beaten egg.

Lay the fish on the pastry, leaving the eggy margins free. Make a slight dent in the fish to keep the sauce in. Pour the sauce on, and immediately flop the pastry over and press down round the edges. Do this with one turnover at a time, or the sauce will escape.

Brush the tops and edges with beaten egg: be careful if your sauce was still warm, as the pastry will then tear easily. If it does, grit your teeth and patch up with scraps from the edges glued with egg.

If you aren't the sort of person who suffers from tearing pastry and leaking sauce, display your perfections by decorating the turnovers prettily with leaves or fish. If you are really talented, you can even fold your pastry to form a fish, and give it fins and eyes. I did that once and was most impressed by my own genius, till I discovered I had forgotten to put the sauce in.

Bake in a hot oven for about 20 minutes, till a rich golden brown.

Salmon

The wild salmon has an instinctive migratory urge which takes it on a
sea journey of up to four years and five thousand miles, before it returns
to its native river to breed. It is this free-swimming migrating stock
which produces the fish crammed lifelong into pens along the Highland
coastline. For that reason, do not buy farmed salmon any more than
you would cage a swallow. Don't be fooled by such optimisms as
"fresh" or "Scottish": if it is not labelled "wild" it is almost certainly
farmed. This applies to the smoked article as well.

In spite of the enthusiastic assurances of marketing, farmed fish
tastes bland, sweetish and subtly disgusting to anyone who is used to
the wild salmon; you would do well to avoid it for that reason alone.

Good salmon is best when cooked gently and minimally in its own
juices. Don't handle it more than necessary, but do scrape all the blood
away from the backbone inside the cavity. If you are cooking a whole
fish or large piece, you don't need to scale it, but if the piece is less than
2 lb (900 g), you had better scrape off the scales, as they will wander
onto the cut surface of the fish.

Either steam the fish on a trivet, or wrap it in kitchen foil (not too
tightly) and cook it in simmering water or in the oven. Forget the
seasonings, the butter and the court bouillon: a fresh wild fish has no
need of these adornments.

Cooking times for these methods are as follows, or at least I hope so.
I quite often get it wrong: you might do better to consult another book
at this point.

Steaming, or simmering in foil:

    1–3 lb (450 g–1.4 kg)   15–25 minutes

    3–5 lb (1.4–2.3 kg)   25–40 minutes

    5–10 lb (2.3–4.5 kg)   40 minutes–1 hour

Baking in foil:

    1–3 lb (450 g–1.4 kg)   30–45 minutes

    3–5 lb (1.4–2.3 kg)   45 minutes–1 hour

    5–10 lb (2.3–4.5 kg)   1–2 hours

The usual sauces for salmon are hollandaise if it is hot or mayonnaise
if it is cold. Nothing could be better than these, along with plenty of
new potatoes. However, if the weather is close, or the rest of the meal
elaborate, I strongly recommend dispensing with a sauce and accompanying the fish, hot or cold, with a separate bowl of Raita, a refreshing
preparation familiar from Indian restaurants.

Raita

½ a cucumber
½ pt (275 ml) yoghurt
1 teaspoon chopped mint
salt, paprika

Chop the cucumber coarsely. I prefer to leave the skin on for colour and taste. Mix in the yoghurt, mint and salt, and sprinkle the top with paprika.

Don't combine the ingredients until just before serving, or it will go watery.

Shellfish

The world is divided into people who adore shellfish and people who are allergic to them. Often one of the first group is married to one of the second. This makes for awkwardness in the planning of set dinner menus. "1 no shellfish" is scribbled by the name of many couples in our bookings register. When other names on the same night bear such legends as "no game", "hates cheese", "avoid citrus", "no tomatoes", etc., the atmosphere in the kitchen is bad and the language foul. Allergies are something of a growth-industry at present. They are particularly popular with well-to-do women. In America even men have them: I find this somehow rather shocking, like my discovery that Marks and Spencers now stock pale pink Y-fronts.

Some people have genuine and very serious allergies, of course, like our black Labrador, Jet. He comes out in enormous lumps if he takes aspirin. If you can imagine a cross between a warthog and a black pudding, you will picture the horror of the effect. The first time it happened, he reduced a perky collie to a quaking wreck simply by staring through his car window.

But to return to shellfish. We can obtain them very fresh from local boats, though every year there are ominous rumours of further decline in stocks, and small inshore boats are pushed out by predators from East and South. But as long as there is still a catch to cook, our concern is to kill it by the most humane method for the particular species.

We freeze scallops whole. Bivalves are less likely than crustaceans to feel pain, but give them the benefit of the doubt. Heat penetration takes quite a long time to kill something as large as a scallop and if you force them open with a knife they palpate for some time afterwards. From common observation, it seems that cold-blooded creatures respond to falling temperatures by a slowing of all physical functions, so I think this is the surest method, insofar as we can be sure. We do the same with langoustines, which being crustaceans are more active. If they found the freezer uncongenial, they would try to escape, as lobsters quite certainly do from boiling water.

We use an electrical stun-tank for lobsters and crabs, but this is hardly practicable for most people. The Universities Federation for Animal Welfare now recommend freezing (in a plastic bag at −10° to −15°C). I have tried this, and it seems to work well. Freeze for at least 5 hours, but not more than 24 hours: after that the texture of the flesh softens. Thaw for only 2−3 hours at kitchen temperature. Boil 10−20 minutes depending on size.

However, I am very doubtful about UFAW's other claim, that fast boiling is a humane death. They assert optimistically that "the lobster should die within 15 seconds", but J. R. Baker's experiments at Oxford tell a different story, almost two minutes of struggling. A method heating the lobster very slowly from cold used to be considered humane, but recently doubts have been cast on it. I used to do this, and I think I would recommend it but very cautiously and only with the following provisos:

(1) Use sea water or water as salty as that.

(2) Use a very heavy pan with a folded towel in the bottom of it.

(3) Heat VERY SLOWLY on a very low heat. The water should take half an hour to become even lukewarm, and the heat should not be raised until it is as hot as a hot bath.

(4) If the lobster becomes more rather than less active at any time, reduce the heat.

A very quick way of killing a lobster is to cut it in half with a stout knife. Have the lobster back up on the table, with the tail outstretched and held in your left hand. Look for the cross-shaped mark at the bottom of the carapace, where it joins the tail. Plunge the knife into this mark and cut quickly up to the head, pushing the knife right through to the belly, and then immediately cut down the middle of the tail. The lobster's nerve ganglia are now destroyed, and it is dead, but be prepared for strong reflex jerks of the two separate halves; macabre, but at less cost of suffering to the lobster than other ways. This method means you can't boil the lobster but you can sauté it or steam it; if you are steaming, lay the halves cut side up, and cook for 10 minutes.

Crabs can be killed almost instantly by stabbing. Arm yourself with a marlin spike or a stout skewer, and pliers. Twist a towel into a ring on the table and lay the crab on that, belly up. Pull back the tail, which will be curled up under the body. You will see a small hole with a groove running back to it. Holding the skewer fractionally tilted towards the head, stick it firmly in at least half an inch (1.25 cm) at this hole. Twist it in all directions. The crab is now paralysed but not dead, so finish it off at once by destroying the other nerve centre, in the head. The easiest way is to put the pliers over the whole face (mouth parts) and close them firmly. If this sounds too horrible (but it is best for the crab) find the small depression between the mouth parts and the two movable plates. Slope the skewer far towards the head and pierce this point by quarter of an inch (6 mm). All this sounds a lot more complicated than it is: if you have a crab in front of you it becomes instantly clear.

Anything is better than buying ready-cooked shellfish to save your-self a squeamish chill. Such creatures will have been killed by boiling crammed together, which prolongs the agony, or by steaming (ever had a steam burn?).

Crab Soufflé

I dread being offered a gift of a bag of crab claws. Amongst lobster fishermen it is a common practice to twist the claws off the crabs which are caught stealing the bait in the creels, and throw the still living bodies back in the sea. So if you see crab claws offered in a restaurant, suspect them.

Don't deal with your first crab before an important dinner party, as they are the most fiddly of all shellfish to prepare. The cooked flesh freezes well for a short time, certainly well enough for made-up dishes.

Kill the crab by either of the suggested methods. Boil it for 10 minutes if it is small, 20 minutes if large. To get out the meat, start by pressing hard on the line running round the under-shell at the top and sides. The middle part of the shell will crack out. Put it to one side. Remove the digestive organs (a small sack at the mouth) and discard. Scrape out the brown meat, but keep it—it lends flavour to the rest. Crack the large claws with a hammer to get out the flesh. If it is a huge crab do the small claws too. Take the piece you lifted out of the underside and use a teaspoon handle to extract the meat from it: it is contained in a series of pockets on each side.

Now you have the crab ready and can continue with the recipe.

The meat of 1 large crab or 6 small
   ones (about 8 inches (20 cm) and
   3 inches (7.5 cm) respectively
   across the carapace)
a little dried tarragon
½ teaspoon French mustard
1 tablespoon Pernod or brandy
a scrape of nutmeg
salt and cayenne pepper
2 oz (50 g) butter
1½ oz (40 g) flour
⅓ pt (190 ml) milk
4 eggs + 1 extra white
Parmesan cheese

Preheat oven to 190°C/375°F and read the general remarks for vegetable soufflés (see pp. 43–5).

Mash the crab meat together with the flavourings. If you have no Pernod or brandy use 2 teaspoons of Worcester sauce.

Make a thick white sauce with the butter, flour and milk. Add it to the crab. Cool this slightly while you grease a 2 pt (1.2 litre) soufflé dish or casserole.

Beat the egg yolks into the crab mixture. Whisk the whites VERY stiff and fold lightly into the rest, turn at once into the dish, sprinkle with the cheese, and bake for 35–40 minutes.

Lobster

Sunday is a short-staffed day with us, so we simplify dinner by cutting out a course. To make it up, the main dish is a whole boiled lobster per person, weather permitting. A windy Saturday means a lobsterless Sunday.

Some people, I think, wish the lobster were less whole, when they see it sitting there in its habit as it lived like the ghost in *Hamlet*, proffering a pot of mayonnaise between outstretched claws.

For remarks on how to kill lobsters see p. 69.

Lobster is quite a robust meat and goes satisfactorily with baked potatoes and a salad. Don't overcook lobster: for a 1 lb (450 g) one, it is enough to bring the water back to a rolling boil for 2 minutes, then turn out the heat and leave the pan covered for a further 10. Even if you are serving them cold, don't cook them too far ahead. They deteriorate quickly and are tasteless chilled, best eaten tepid and wetly juicy.

Lobster Mayonnaise

Here is the strong-flavoured mayonnaise I prefer for lobster. Use only first-pressing unrefined oils.

    1 egg yolk
    ¼ teaspoon salt
    ½ teaspoon mustard (French or
        English)
    1 tablespoon wine vinegar
    almost ½ pt (275 ml) of mixed
        olive oil and sunflower oil

To prevent curdling, have all the ingredients at the same temperature, add some of the acid with the egg yolk, and add the oil VERY slowly at first. This applies to any mayonnaise.

Put the egg yolk in a small basin with the salt, mustard and 2 teaspoons of the vinegar. Beat or whisk till lightish in colour.

Mix the oils in a small jug that pours well. Drip in a drop at a time, a little more if you are using a rotary whisk and it can trickle slowly down the blades. Beat between each drop and after 10 such additions add splashes rather than drops. Once the mixture thickens you can add the rest of the oil quite recklessly. If it gets too stiff, add some of the vinegar. Test for sharpness: you may like more or less vinegar.

A more bland mayonnaise suitable for vegetables or fish can be made with less mustard and all sunflower oil. Lemon juice can be substituted for vinegar. I never add sugar to mayonnaise but some people like it. If you do, put it in at the beginning, as it (and salt) remain gritty if added at the end.

Langoustines

These are also known as Dublin Bay prawns or scampi. In North West Scotland they are simply prawns. They have long nippy claws like lobsters. In the larger ones of six inches (15 cm) upwards there is a fair bit of meat in these claws, and the body contains tasty yellowy green liver which is good in small quantities. So it is worth serving the big specimens whole, but the diners must be prepared to use animal methods to extract the goodies. Sometimes you can watch an otter perched on a rock, scrunching and sucking at a crab, with eyes half-closed in bliss, and this is the way to eat whole langoustines —though you needn't sit on a rock.

Langoustines with Sour Cream and Herb Dressing

Langoustines need very little cooking: it is enough to bring the water back to the boil. Allow five large ones per person for a starter, ten for a main course. Provide a finger bowl, a plate for débris, and the following dressing.

Sour cream and herb dressing
4¼ pt (150 ml) double cream
juice of ½ lemon
¼ pt (150 ml) yoghurt

2 tablespoons fresh herbs, chopped
1-inch (2.5 cm) long piece of
    cucumber
salt

Whip the cream with the lemon juice till stiff. Add the yoghurt, the finely-chopped cucumber, and the herbs. Parsley and chives should definitely be included, with smaller quantities of dill, fennel, tarragon, chervil, mint or lovage, as available. Salt cautiously.

You can use cultured sour cream instead of cream with lemon juice. If you like a very rich dressing, use extra cream instead of yoghurt.

Spiced Langoustines

This quantity is enough for a starter for six people. For a main course, double everything, and serve with rice or a flat wholewheat bread. Though bogus, this tastes Indian enough to be part of a curry meal.

30 langoustines
1 bay leaf
1 tablespoon fennel seeds
1 tablespoon coriander seeds
1 teaspoon turmeric
½ teaspoon chilli powder (more or
    less according to taste)

2 cloves garlic
½ teaspoon salt
juice of 2 lemons
2 tablespoons finely chopped mint
4 oz (100 g) butter

Grind all the spices together. Crush the garlic with salt. Melt the butter and add to it everything except the langoustines.

With a very sharp knife, slit the belly shell lengthwise. Prise it apart slightly (a prickly job) and stuff in a bit of spiced butter. Do this to all the langoustines and lay them stretched out belly down, on a baking tray. Paste the remaining spiced butter over their backs. If you have the patience, stab each shell a few times first.

It is best to leave the shellfish in a cool place for several hours at this point, though not essential. Bake them in a hot oven for 5 minutes. Don't waste the juices—pour them over when you serve.

Mussels

We used to go to endless lengths to clean mussels, even turning them in the cement mixer to knock off barnacles. Now I cook them barnacles and all: the grot comes off when the liquor boils up, and what doesn't rubs off easily. The beards often disappear too, or can be easily tweaked out by pinching the shell closed. Of course, you have to strain the juice through muslin or a teatowel before using it.

Mussels being small, they open quickly in heat, so probably this is no worse a way for them to die than by freezing. You may snort at the idea of a mussel feeling pain, but if it doesn't, why does it bother to form pearls round uncomfortable bits of grit? Mussels do this just like oysters, though the pearls are not of commercial size.

If you gather your own mussels, be very careful. They thrive on sewage, but you won't. I have only once gathered mussels within sight of human habitation. They were recommended as particularly plump and juicy by strong-stomached friends. I was spectacularly ill afterwards, though it may have been quantity rather than quality that did it.

Nowadays our shores are festooned with farmed mussels. I don't think the mussels mind it, but the product is unpleasantly sweet and flabby. They feed naturally, but more intensively than wild mussels, as they are not intertidal; so they are as pudgy and bloated as dyspeptic businessmen.

Good mussels have a distinct and strong flavour, and go well with many vegetables—onions, garlic, tomatoes, peppers, fennel. They need a wine which is tasty but not too subtle. I prefer a good Muscadet, and recommend broaching it for the sauce of the next recipe.

Mussels with Fennel

3 quarts mussels
¼ pt (150 ml) dry white wine
1 large bulb fennel
1 medium onion
1½ oz (40 g) butter
1 oz (25 g) flour
3 tablespoons double cream

Slice the onion and fennel finely, reserving some of the green fennel tops for garnish. Stew them in the butter over a gentle heat, covered, till tender. This will take up to 15 minutes.

Wash the mussels to get rid of loose grit. Discard any that stay open when tapped. Put them in a covered pan with the wine. Set this on a high heat. As soon as this boils up and over the mussels, they will open.

Strain the mussel liquor into a jug. Discard one shell from each mussel and keep the rest warm.

Stir the flour into the fennel and make a sauce by adding 1 pt (570 ml) of the mussel liquor. Simmer for 2 minutes.

Dish the mussels into shallow bowls. Add the cream and chopped fennel tops to the sauce, and ladle over the mussels. Serve with warm bread to soak up the sauce.

Mussels Provençales

This is very quick and tasty, but only Provençal for want of a better name. It makes a good sauce for pasta.

> 3 quarts mussels
> ¼ pt (150 ml) water
> 2 tablespoons olive oil
> 1 red pepper
> 3 cloves garlic, crushed
> 1 large tin of tomatoes
> 1 tablespoon tomato purée
> 1 tablespoon chopped parsley
> 1 tablespoon Pernod or ferocious
>   red wine

Cook the mussels as for the preceding recipe, but using water instead of wine. For this dish shell the mussels completely. Strain ¼ pt (150 ml) of the liquid, and discard the rest.

Slice the pepper finely. Simmer it with all the other ingredients, uncovered, for about 10 minutes, or till the liquid has boiled in. Cautiously add the mussel liquor, but don't get it too salty—use some water if it is very salty. Replace the shelled mussels in the sauce and reheat.

If you omit the mussel liquor, this makes a nice pizza topping.

Scallops

The well-educated call these bivalves scollops and correct me firmly when I say scallops. In Harris they are always called clams anyway. The biggest and freshest are got by diving, and these select shellfish cost half as much again as the dredged catch. Clam-divers are invested with high earnings and an air of romance—till something goes wrong. It is a physically taxing and very risky career. We always try to buy from divers. Not only are their scallops finer, smelling of the sea rather than bilge-water, but they do no harm to the sea-bed. A dredge claws the bottom like a giant harrow, tearing out every scallop, large and tiny, whole and broken, and devastating the entire plant and animal community of the sea bed. Regeneration takes years, if indeed it ever happens.

Most classic recipes for "coquilles" are too rich and cloying to use with really fresh scallops though convenient for disguising the aforementioned bilge-water flavour if it is pronounced. The recipes given below are very simple.

Scallops in oatmeal

The Scots use oatmeal as a coating for various types of fish. Herring in oatmeal, trout in oatmeal, so why not scallops in oatmeal? Less bother than egg and breadcrumbs, and more interesting too.

For the scallops:	For the garnish:
18–24 scallops	1 lemon
about 4 oz (100 g) fine oatmeal	1 large tomato
3–4 oz (75–100 g) butter	shredded lettuce

For the scallops:
If the scallops have been frozen they will be very easy to shell. Using a stout knife, prise the two halves apart near the hinge. Discard every thing except the round white bit and the bright orange coral. In addition cut off the very opaque fibres down one side of the white, and the tough grey-brown piece at the thicker end of the coral. Save 6 of the deep shells. Cut the white part into two or three rounds, ½ inch (1.25 cm) thick. Leave the corals whole. (Sometimes there are none.) Using one hand only (it's a sticky job) dip the pieces in the dry oatmeal. Start frying with just 1 oz (25 g) of the butter, adding more as necessary.

Cook the scallops gently for about 5 minutes on each side—the flesh turns pale and opaque when it is ready.

For the garnish:

Cut the lemon and the tomato each into 6 sections. Divide the lettuce between the shells. Dish the scallops onto this, decorate with the lemon and tomato and serve before it gets uniformly lukewarm.

These are fine as they are, but if you want a sauce, use a sharp piquant one—no eggs or cream—totally cholesterol-free. This is what I usually serve:

Spicy Tomato Sauce

A lump of tamarind pulp (about
   1-inch (2.5 cm) cube)
½ teacup boiling water
2 star anise *or* 1 teaspoon aniseed
   or fennel seed
1 teaspoon black peppercorns
1 tablespoon coriander seed
1 lb (450 g) tomatoes
1 medium onion
salt

Put the tamarind in the cup of hot water and leave to soak. (If you don't have tamarind, mix the juice of 1 lemon and 2 teaspoons dark brown sugar.)

Grind the spices and put them in a saucepan over medium heat till they darken and smell aromatic. Add the onion and tomatoes roughly cut up, and stir well. Paddle the tamarind in the water with your fingers, discard the seeds and husks, and add the softened pulp or the lemon juice to the tomato mixture. Simmer till the onion is soft—20–30 minutes. Strain by pushing through a sieve with the back of a ladle: this is very easy if you liquidise the mixture first. Add salt to taste and a little brown sugar if it is too sour for you, but remember the scallops are sweetish in flavour.

Scallops in yoghurt

I can never decide whether this recipe is a flower of my genius or a
disgusting aberration, but many diners have raved about it. Others
have said nothing. . . .

>   18–24 scallops
>   juice of 1 lemon
>   salt, nutmeg and freshly ground
>   black pepper
>   2 oz (50 g) unsalted butter
>   1 teaspoon arrowroot slaked in
>   1 tablespoon water (optional)
>   ¼ pt (150 ml) yoghurt

Prepare the scallops and slice into rings. Lay on a baking sheet and
sprinkle with the lemon juice and seasonings. Use very little salt—
¼ teaspoon at most. Leave for half an hour.

Melt the butter in a wide pan, and put in the scallops and any juice
they have exuded. Mix gently, cover, and cook just till opaque, turning
once or twice. Don't let the collecting juices boil, or the scallop will
toughen.

Remove the scallops with a slotted spoon and keep warm. Turn up
the heat and boil the juice fiercely, uncovered, till it is well reduced. If
you are a purist, boil grimly till you have only about a teacupful of
syrupy liquid left. If you find this too tedious, reduce to twice that and
thicken with the arrowroot.

Take the pan off the heat. Dish up the scallops, either in the deep
shells or in a bowl. Add the yoghurt to the juice in the pan, mixing well,
but do *not* reheat, or it will curdle. Pour this sauce over the scallops.

Seafood Pie or Gougère

I make these when I end up with quantities of this and that too small to
feed a whole dining room. For the pastry or gougère crust, follow the
instructions under Turnover of Sole (p. 64) or Gougère of Mushrooms
and Peppers (p. 54). For hearty eaters you will need to double the
gougère paste quantities to serve 6 as a main course, but the filling
ingredients given below are enough for 6. For a cheaper dish you can
substitute firm white fish for the lobster.

For the filling:
6 scallops
12 langoustines *or* 24 prawns
1 small lobster
20 mussels
½ pt (275 ml) dry white wine *or*
    wine and water
1 bay leaf
1 small onion
2-inch (5 cm) strip lemon peel

2 oz (50 g) butter
2 oz (50 g) flour
1 tablespoon chopped parsley
½ teaspoon dried tarragon, thyme
    or basil
salt and cayenne pepper
1 teaspoon French mustard *or*
    2 tablespoons sherry
3 tablespoons cream

Cut the scallops into rounds. Shell the langoustines or prawns and the lobster, and put the shells in a large pan with the wine, bay leaf, sliced onion and lemon peel. Bring to the boil. Lay the mussels in their shells on top, cover the pan and boil for 2 minutes.

Remove the mussels from their shells, cut the lobster meat into chunks, and mix all the shellfish together in a bowl. You don't want people sulking because someone got all lobster while another had all mussels.

Strain the shellfish stock into a jug and make up to ¾ pt (425 ml) with milk or water if necessary.

Make a roux with the butter and flour. Add the stock and beat till smooth. Add all the remaining ingredients and taste. It should be highly seasoned.

For the pie:

Roll out the pastry to fit a large pie dish or 2 small ones. Lay the shellfish in the bottom, pour on the cooled sauce, and place the pastry over, gluing it to the dish with beaten egg at the edge. Brush the top with egg, and make a small hole in the middle. A ribbon of pastry over or under the lid at the edge helps to prevent shrinking and oozing. Bake for about 20 minutes in a moderately hot oven till golden brown.

For the gougère:

Bake the crust as directed. 10 minutes before it is ready, bring the sauce to boiling point. Drop in the shellfish, and cook very gently —below a simmer—till the crust comes out. Dollop the mixture into the centre of the gougère and serve at once.

The shellfish mixture can also be served over rice or another grain.

Game and other Meat

I have called this section "Game and other meat", because if I have to cook meat I prefer to use game. This is not from any liking for huntin' and shootin': in fact, I am bemused by the excitement sportsmen find in the chase. I can remotely imagine rejoicing in an unarmed victory over a grizzly bear or a rabid wolf, but where is the thrill in vanquishing a clawless, fangless, oblivious herbivore with a high velocity bullet? Be that as it may, at least the victims have led relatively unconfined lives and are hit before they know it's coming.

A rueful sportsman told us the following tale. He had arrived in Harris for fishing, having just been presented with some grouse on the mainland. These he thrust into the hands of his bed-and-breakfast lady, instructing her to cook them for his supper. After many hungry hours flogging the loch and anticipating dinner, he arrived back. There was an odd smell in the house—not entirely appetising—but he seated himself at the supper table. The landlady appeared, smiling to herself, bearing in the grouse—thoroughly cooked, but cooked guts, feathers and all.

Well done, you bad old lady! For what reason on earth should she pluck the Sassenach's grouse? A fresh hen is unpleasant enough, but a high grouse is abominable.

Pheasant

Pheasants have only recently been successfully introduced in Lewis, and for the first couple of years they tasted suspiciously like chicken. As there are no cornfields and no woods, the poor things hung around waiting for handouts of grain. Plantations have by now improved their lifestyle.

Pheasants are surprisingly meaty and one bird will serve three. Don't try to gnaw your way through the drumsticks: they are very sinewy. Boil them up with onion, carrot and celery and make a soup.

Pheasant with Apples and Rosemary

This is similar to the classic Faisan à la Normande, but the sauce is more robust, with a slightly bitter pungency from the rosemary.

2 pheasants	4 tart eating apples, *or* 2 sweet ones
2 oz (50 g) butter	and 2 cooking apples
2 medium onions	3 tablespoons brandy
4 4-inch-long (10 cm) sprigs	½ teaspoon salt
rosemary	2 tablespoons cream

Trim excess fat round the vents of the pheasants. Put ½ oz (15 g) of butter and a sprig of rosemary in the cavity of each.

Chop the onions and sauté in the rest of the butter till golden. Core the apples and peel them, or not, as you like. Cut them in quarters and turn them in the butter with the onion. Scrape all this into the bottom of a large lidded casserole or roaster. Add the remaining sprigs of rosemary. Place the pheasants on top and sprinkle with salt.

Warm the brandy in a small pan, ignite it, and pour it quickly over the pheasants. While it is still blazing, put on the lid. Cook in a moderate oven for 60 minutes, basting two or three times. You may need to add a little water.

Dish up and carve the pheasants, and keep warm. Taste the apple mixture, adding salt, and sugar or lemon juice if it seems to need it. Remove the scraggy stalks of the rosemary but leave the leaves in. Add cream if you like it, and pour this sauce over the sliced pheasant.

It is a horrible colour. If you have plenty of rosemary, lay a criss-cross of fresh sprigs over the top. Otherwise avert your eyes. The taste is fine, anyway.

Pot-roasted Pheasant

If the pheasants are tough, this is a good method.

2 pheasants
2 medium onions
2 medium carrots
3 stalks celery
1 oz (50 g) butter
salt
a bay leaf, a sprig of thyme and a
    strip of lemon peel
¼ pt (150 ml) tasty white wine or
    feeble port
1 teaspoon flour
¼ pt (150 ml) double cream
redcurrant or quince jelly or lemon
    juice—optional
chopped parsley to garnish

Trim excess fat from the vents of the pheasants. Chop the vegetables coarsely and brown them lightly in the butter. Remove them with a draining spoon to the bottom of a large lidded casserole and brown the pheasants in the same pan.

Lay the bay leaf, etc., on the vegetables and sprinkle with the salt. Put the pheasants on top, breast down, and pour the wine over them. Cook slowly, covered, on the stove top or in a slowish oven for 1½–2 hours. Turn the birds over and stir the vegetables occasionally.

Remove and carve the pheasants and keep warm. Drain most of the fat from the vegetables and stir in the flour over heat. Add a little stock or water if necessary to make a thickish sauce. Adjust the seasoning—if you used wine you may want to add a little redcurrant or quince jelly; if port, a squeeze of lemon juice. Stir in the cream, reheat without boiling, and pour the vegetable mixture into the centre of the serving platter. Sprinkle with parsley, as this one isn't a nice colour either.

Pheasant with Oatmeal Stuffing

To roast a pheasant, rub the breast well with butter, put an onion and a knob of butter inside, and roast for 40–50 minutes in a moderately hot oven, basting several times. The following recipe is for a traditional Scottish poultry stuffing. If you fill the birds with this, clean out the cavity very well first with kitchen paper, and increase the cooking time by 10 minutes. This quantity will do two pheasants.

Oatmeal stuffing
3 oz (75 g) dripping or white
    cooking fat—not lard from a
    block
1 medium onion
6 oz (175 g) fine or medium
    oatmeal
salt and pepper
¼ pt (150 ml) water

Chop the onion and fry till it begins to brown in the dripping. Put in the oatmeal and cook, stirring, till it turns pale and then begins to darken slightly. Remove from the heat, add salt, pepper and water.

Venison

We don't hang our venison long. We get stags in August, when the weather is damp and mild and putrefaction is in the air. On the seventh day the worm fastened on Ea-bani, and so on a Harris stag. We cut it up hastily and stuff it in the freezer. Hinds, shot in January and February, would last a little longer hanging, but we have no taste for decay and usually don't keep them either. Good red deer venison tastes of the heather it fed on, and hanging is more useful for tenderising than flavouring it. Venison freezes better than other meat, which is just as well when you have two hundredweights at once, and freezing makes it more tender; but it is never as good as fresh.

Try to get a well-nourished beast, but when you are preparing the meat, trim away all the fat, particularly if you are dealing with a stag's hindquarters. The stuff has a pungent odour which may turn on a hind, but it will hardly delight your dinner-guests. You will, of course, have to add other fats to make up. I find butter best.

Roast Venison with Rosemary Jelly

The best cuts for roasting are the saddle, the rump, and the top of the haunch. Weigh the meat after trimming, and calculate the cooking time at 10 minutes to the pound and 10 minutes over for medium rare, in a moderately hot oven.

To flavour and baste a 4–5 lb (1.8–2.2 kg) roast, you will need:

  10 juniper berries
  1 teaspoon dried rosemary
  ½ teaspoon salt
  2–3 oz (50–75 g) butter
  4 sprigs bog myrtle or thyme

Crush the juniper berries and dried rosemary with the salt, and rub this all over the meat. Butter the roasting tin thickly and squash the rest of the butter over the top of the meat and into any crevices. Baste very frequently.

You will probably have no excess fat in the gravy. Deglaze the roasting tin with a little venison stock or water, and 2 tablespoons of port. Failing port, use wine and a teaspoon of a tart jelly. Strain the gravy as it will have bits of herb-stalk in it.

Rosemary Jelly

My mother-in-law drew my attention to this lovely preserve, and now makes mine for me. Mine is murky and musty—hers is clear and fragrant. It is the ideal accompaniment with game, and also good with mature mutton.

You can use your usual apple jelly recipe, and to the apples and water add a good-sized branch of rosemary, which stews along with them. Don't try using dried rosemary; it is lacking in the essential oil which imparts the fresh flavour.

If you don't have a favourite jelly recipe, here is the method in full.

The amount of sugar required and the final yield varies depending on the condition of the fruit.

  6 lb (2.8 kg) cooking apples or
    windfalls
  water to cover
  a few branches of rosemary
  granulated sugar

Remove bad pieces from the apples but do not peel or core. Cut into thick slices, put in a jelly pan with the rosemary, and just cover with water. Bring to the boil and simmer for about 1 hour, till the liquid is reduced by one third.

Strain the pulp through a jelly bag for at least an hour, till the pulp is dry. Measure the resulting juice and return to the rinsed-out pan with 1 lb (450 g) sugar for every half pint (275 ml) of juice.

Bring to the boil, stirring to dissolve the sugar. Boil rapidly till setting point is reached (probably about 10 minutes). Test a little by dropping it on a cold plate. Let it cool and if it wrinkles when the plate is tilted, it is ready.

Pour into dry, warm jars and cover.

Venison Chops with Vermouth

This method would also work with elderly grouse, following the slower cooking after initial browning.

6 thick venison chops
2 oz (50 g) butter
1 smallish onion
6 juniper berries
1 × 4-inch (10 cm) sprig of rosemary

½ teaspoon dried thyme
½ teaspoon salt
¼ pt (150 ml) dry Vermouth
½ oz (15 g) flour
¼ pt (150 ml) game stock or water
1 tablespoon sultanas

Trim the chops thoroughly. Chop the onion finely and brown with the meat in the butter over a high heat. Remove the onions and chops to an ovenproof dish. Lay them in a single layer.

Crush the herbs with the salt to release the aromatic oils, and sprinkle over the chops. Swill the Vermouth over the meat. To the butter in the browning pan, add the flour, scraping well to incorporate it. Stir in the stock or water, add the sultanas, and simmer for 2 minutes. Pour this over the chops.

Either (1) Leave the dish uncovered and bake in a hot oven for 10 minutes, turning once. The meat will be rare and the sauce syrupy.

Or (2) Cover with greaseproof paper or a lid and bake in a slow oven for 40 minutes, basting once or twice. The meat will be brown right through and drier, but it will have absorbed the sweetish flavour of the sauce.

A julienne of celery and potato goes well with this (see recipe p. 100).

Civet of Venison

This is a glorified stew, really, richly flavoured and aromatic. It also makes an excellent pie filling. Shoulder is the best cut to use. The really stringy ends of the beast—neck and lower legs—should be used for the next recipe.

2–2½ lb (.9–1.1 kg) venison (weight excludes bone)
3 oz (75 g) bacon
1 tablespoon olive oil
1 oz (25 g) butter
2 large onions
1 medium carrot
6 oz (175 g) mushrooms
1 oz (25 g) flour
½ bottle full-bodied (even blowsy) red wine
1 wineglass brandy or whisky
1 bay leaf
2-inch (5 cm) strip lemon peel
½ teaspoon dried thyme
3 cloves garlic
6 juniper berries
venison stock or water
To garnish:
triangles of fried bread or puff pastry or a few mushrooms

Trim all the sinewy and scraggy bits off the meat. It is convenient to have a dog sitting beside you who will obligingly remove the waste before you notice your own extravagance. Cut what is left into 1-inch (2.5 cm) cubes.

Cut the bacon into small pieces and sizzle it in the oil and butter till the fat runs out. Get the pan very hot and brown the meat.

Chop the onions and carrots coarsely and the mushroom stalks finely. (Reserve the mushroom caps.) Add to the pan of meat and cook, stirring, for a couple of minutes.

Stir in the flour, and follow that with the brandy, wine and herbs. Crush the garlic and juniper berries with a pinch of salt and add that too. Mix well, and simmer gently till the meat is tender—about 2 hours. Check several times to make sure the liquid has not evaporated. If your dog was taking a nap earlier, you could make stock with the trimmings and use that to top up with. Otherwise use water.

10 minutes before serving, test for salt. If the bacon was mild you may need more. Put in the mushroom caps at this stage and another splash of wine if it was unassertive.

You can garnish with triangles of fried bread or puff pastry; a few more small fried mushrooms; or just plenty of parsley, and hope no one notices you didn't do the other things.

Venison Pudding

This is a very substantial and warming winter dish. If possible, take the meat off the bones yourself: and use them to make stock which is really needed for this recipe.

For the filling:
1½–2 lb (700–900 g) so-called "stewing venison" or 3–4 lb (1.4–1.8 kg) on the bone
2 oz (50 g) dripping or butter
2 large onions
1 medium carrot
2 stalks celery
¼ lb (100 g) turnip or swede
½ oz (15 g) flour
1 pt (570 ml) venison stock, *or* ½ pt (275 ml) stock and ½ pt (275 ml) beer

1–2 teaspoons French mustard
1 tablespoon Worcester sauce or mushroom ketchup
1 teaspoon brown sugar
½ teaspoon dried savory or mixed herbs
salt and pepper
For the suet crust:
8 oz (225 g) self-raising flour
½ teaspoon salt
4 oz (100 g) shredded suet
water

For the filling:

Remove the bones and the toughest-looking bits of sinew. Smuggle these trimmings into a pan while the dog is out chasing cats and boil up with 1½ pt (825 ml) water. Simmer for 1 hour or till you are ready for it.

Cut the bits of venison—I'm assuming it's scraggy—into roughly 1-inch (2.5 cm) cubes. Brown them in the fat.

Dice the vegetables, not too small, and brown them with the meat. Sprinkle in the flour. Add ⅓ pt (200 ml) of the liquid and all the seasonings and simmer till the meat is tender. This will take about 3–4 hours and can be done a day or so ahead. Check every half hour for sticking and top up the liquid as necessary. Check the seasoning—it should be well-flavoured. Cool the stew somewhat.

For the suet crust:

Mix the flour, salt and shredded suet. Add enough cold water to make a soft scone-like dough. Roll out about ⅔ of it very lightly on a floured surface and piece this together to line a 2 pt (1.2 litre) pudding basin, thinly but thoroughly—about ¼ inch (6 mm) thick. Pat the remaining third out into a round to fit the top of the basin.

Fill the lined basin with the stew, using a draining spoon. Leave a good deal of the gravy in the pan: the filling should be moist but not swimming. Place the top crust over, pinching it on to the inner crust.

Cover the pudding with a double layer of greaseproof paper, greased, and with a 2-inch (5 cm) pleat down the centre to allow for

87

swelling. Tie it up firmly—it's a good plan to anchor the paper under the basin rim with an elastic band before tying the string. The band perishes with the steam, but does no harm. Trim the ends of the paper and string so that they won't soak up the water. Set the basin on a steamer or in 1½ inches (3.75 cm) of boiling water, cover, and cook for 1–1½ hours. Don't let the water touch the paper, boil dry, or go off the boil.

Heat up the rest of the gravy and serve it separately, with mashed potatoes, and a green vegetable.

If you can't be bothered fiddling with a pudding basin, make the stew and pastry as directed. Pull the pastry into 12 lumps to make dumplings, and cook them in the simmering stew for 15 minutes.

Lamb

Out of force of habit, and to allay prejudice, we feature "lamb" on our menus, but in fact we can hardly ever get lamb in Harris. The youngest carcases we ever lay hands on are fourteen months, and they only weigh between 20 and 30 pounds. They are difficult to get hold of, because no one sees the sense of killing a beast at that weight that might grow twice as heavy, with time. It's like persuading the grower of prize vegetable marrows to harvest courgettes. The preferred local style is a nice fat wedder—a wedder being a castrated ram of 2 or more years old. They are good mutton, but doubtful lamb. The three recipes following make use of robust flavours for this reason. Try them, and your lamb will be dressed as mutton.

Lamb with Apricots

This is an adaptation of a middle eastern tradition. If the apricots are sweet, add the juice and rind of half a lemon, but it won't be as good.

    4 lb (1.8 kg) leg of lamb
    2 oz (50 g) butter
    1 medium onion
    4 oz (100 g) sour dried apricots
    1-inch (2.5 cm) piece of cinnamon
        stick
    ½ pint (275 ml) water
    salt and pepper

Chop the onion finely and brown it and the leg of lamb lightly in the butter. Transfer these to a lidded casserole, preferably metal, and add all the other ingredients. Bring to a simmer, and then cook, covered, in a very moderate oven for 2–2½ hours. Turn the meat twice and add more water as necessary. You should end up with the meat pulling away easily from the bone at the shank end, and a mush of darkened but still juicy apricots, without much liquid.

Rice cooked in the following manner makes an attractive border to the platter of lamb.

Rice with Pine Kernels

You could use any long-grain rice, but Basmati is very good-tempered. I never bother with washing it or any other fancy procedure, and it still cooks dry and separate.

    12 oz (350 g) Basmati rice
    ½ teaspoon saffron strands
    ½ teaspoon salt
    water
    2 oz (50 g) butter
    2 oz (50 g) pine kernels
    2 oz (50 g) raisins

Put the rice in a jug or bowl to judge its volume. Empty it into a saucepan and add just over twice its volume of water. Add the saffron and salt, stir and bring to the boil. Turn the heat right down and cook tightly covered for 10 minutes. Remove from the heat, still covered, and leave for a further 5–10 minutes.

Heat the butter in a small saucepan till just browning. Add the pine kernels and raisins and stir till the raisins puff up. Serve the rice with this mixture dribbled over the top.

Lamb with Haricots

This is not meant to be "gigot aux haricots" so don't judge it accordingly.

    8 oz (225 g) dried haricot beans
    2 pt (1.2 l) water
    1 bay leaf
    4 cloves garlic
    4 lb (1.8 kg) leg of lamb
    4 oz (100 g) smoked fat bacon
    1 tablespoon olive oil
    2 medium onions
    1 lb (450 g) tomatoes
    1 teaspoon dried oregano or a few
        sprigs fresh marjoram
    salt

Boil the haricots with the water, bay leaf and 1 clove of garlic till half cooked—about 1–1½ hours depending on whether you soaked them first.

Chop the bacon and sizzle it in the oil till the fat comes out. Add the chopped onions and the remaining garlic, crushed.

Skin and chop the tomatoes. If seeds bother you take them out and strain the juice from them. Add the tomatoes to the bacon and onion.

Put all this in a covered casserole or roaster and add the haricots and their liquid. Add the herbs and salt and stir well. Put in the meat, bring to the boil, cover and cook gently for 2½ hours. Turn the meat and make sure the beans don't dry out.

If any beans are left, purée them and serve as a soup with croûtons next day.

Stuffed Shoulder of Lamb

This is a light fresh-tasting stuffing, very summery. It is also good with breast of lamb.

4–5 lb (1.8–2.3 kg) shoulder of
  lamb
For the stuffing:
2 oz (50 g) butter
4 oz (100 g) breadcrumbs
1 tablespoon chopped parsley
1 teaspoon dried thyme (or
  2 teaspoons if fresh)
1 teaspoon dried marjoram (or
  2 teaspoons if fresh)
grated rind and juice of 1 lemon
salt
For roasting:
1 oz (25 g) butter
2 sprigs rosemary

Bone out the lamb and trim the fat.

Melt the butter for the stuffing and add all the other ingredients to it. Stuff this into all the cavities in the lamb. Tie it up as well as you can: don't worry if it's untidy, but try to arrange it so that the muscle fibres all run more or less parallel.

Use ½ oz (15 g) butter to grease a roasting tin. Lay the meat on it with the rosemary and the clove of garlic split in half underneath. Smear the rest of the butter over the top of the meat. Roast in a moderately hot oven for about 1¼ hours, or longer if you like the meat well done. Baste several times.

Make gravy in the usual way and serve fresh mint sauce alongside.

Mint Sauce

¼ pt (150 ml) (loose measure) mint
  leaves
1 teaspoon sugar
1 tablespoon wine vinegar
½ tablespoon water

Put everything in a blender for 10 seconds. It will probably look frothy but it is much less work than chopping and produces a very intense flavour and colour. Use the day it is made.

Offal

The next two recipes are for offal. We never use it as part of our set dinner menu, as it is very common for people to have an aversion to it, but if you aren't one of these squeamish ones, it is all good stuff, cheap and nourishing.

These recipes date from the time when we were renovating the house before opening as a hotel. We were very hard up, and constantly hungry. We virtually lived on sheep's innards donated by a kindly butcher friend, and I evolved many ways of cooking them to vary our diet. Nowadays, our dog is the only meat-eater left in the family, and he is still catered for by the same kind friend. On holiday, I buy him offal on the grounds that no animal is killed specially for its insides. After about three days in one place, I get miserably embarrassed about revisiting the village butcher for a daily parcel of one pound of heart. I feel I am suspected of sinister practices. But Jet gulps it down with the ecstatic relish of an Aztec priest.

Casserole of Heart with Prunes

Hearts have a much more meaty texture than other offal and require long, slow cooking. If you slice them first, you can remove the unappetising stringy bits inside and the signs of fatty degeneration around the top. I think they are best in an aromatic sweetish gravy like the one below. I leave the spices whole—you could grind them, but don't use ready ground. Serve with plenty of rice or fried potatoes to soak up the tasty sauce.

5 or 6 sheep's hearts—about 2 lb (900 g) weight
1 large onion
2 oz (50 g) dripping or oil
1 oz (25 g) flour
1 dessertspoon paprika
3 cloves garlic
a 3-inch (7.5 cm) piece of lemon or orange rind
a 1-inch (2.5 cm) stick of cinnamon

a blade of mace
12 black peppercorns
2 bay leaves
1 teaspoon celery salt
1 glass red wine or juice of half a lemon
¾ pint (425 ml) water
12 large prunes or 18 small
1 green pepper

Slice onion and hearts and brown them in the fat. Stir in the flour and paprika and let it sizzle for a minute. Add everything else except the prunes and green pepper and simmer for 2½ hours, topping up the water if it boils in.

Chop the pepper and add it with the prunes.

Cook for a further 45 minutes. The prunes will absorb a lot of water, so check this.

Liver with Sage and Orange

It was always sheep's liver I had to hand, and I made some nasty mistakes with it. For instance, we had sheep's liver pâté, the most disgusting way of wasting butter next to the EEC butter mountain; and sheep's liver soup, reminiscent of sawdust suspended in sheep's pee. But one or two recipes were an unqualified success, for instance this one. Serve with spaghetti.

For the sauce:
1 tablespoon olive oil
1 small onion
2 cloves garlic
½ teaspoon salt
½ teaspoon sugar
a sprig of fresh thyme or a pinch of
    dried
2 teaspoons flour
1 tablespoon tomato purée
juice and grated rind of 1 large
    orange
¼ pt (150 ml) water
(2 teaspoons capers—optional)

For the liver:
1½ lb (675 g) liver
1 tablespoon chopped fresh sage or
    1 teaspoon dried
½ oz (15 g) butter

For the sauce:
Chop the onion, crush the garlic with the salt and sugar, and sauté in the oil till tender. Add all the other ingredients and simmer for one minute. Take off the heat.
For the liver:
Slice the liver fairly thinly and fry lightly in the butter with the sage. Don't overcook—it should still show a bead of pink juice when pricked.

Pour over the sauce and reheat to simmering point. Serve at once.

Cereals and Vegetable Side-dishes

The quantities given are for small helpings on the side for 6 people, but in fact many of these dishes can form a simple vegetarian main course for 2. They are what we usually eat ourselves for supper after the guests have finished, so there is always a strong element of self-interest in my choice and preparation of these items.

Cereals

There is not much to be said about cereals except that they are not cornflakes. I suspect the British prefer roast potatoes, but I occasionally use some other juice-catcher, especially with fish.

Buckwheat with Cucumber

Buckwheat is not wheat at all—it is a relative of rhubarb. It is stuffed with minerals and bursting with protein. It is highly esteemed by the Japanese, and in Eastern Europe, buckwheat kasha was as porridge to the Scots. I'm not sure how much I like it, personally, but there's something about it—I keep trying it again.

4 oz (100 g) buckwheat
1 egg (optional)
½ pt (275 ml) water
1 cucumber
1 tablespoon snipped chives

salt
1 oz (25 g) butter
¼ pt (150 ml) yoghurt or sour
  cream

94

Beat the egg and mix it into the buckwheat. (This keeps the grains separate, but you can omit the egg if you don't mind stickiness.) Put this in a heated pan and stir till it looks dry. Pour on the water, cover and simmer till tender—about 20 minutes.

Cut the cucumber in half-inch (1.25 cm) chunks or thereabouts. Stew it gently in the butter with the salt and chives, covered, till just cooked—about 4 minutes.

Mix the cucumber into the buckwheat and pour the yoghurt or sour cream over the top.

Bulgar (or Bulghur, or Cracked Wheat)

The Bulgarians gave their name to this method of preparing wheat grain, and also to buggery, but as far as I know there is no connection between the two practices.

The wheat is sold ready husked, boiled, dried and cracked. It may be fine or coarse—use fine for Tabbouleh, the Middle Eastern salad, and coarse for a plain steamed grain or a pilaff. In any form it is delicious and easy to deal with. It has a bland yet warm flavour which goes well with all vegetables, shellfish and lamb.

Burghul Pilaff

2 oz (50 g) butter
1 large onion
1 red pepper or ½ lb (225 g)
   tomatoes
½ lb (225 g) coarse cracked wheat
¾ pt (425 ml) water
salt and pepper

Chop the onion and fry in the butter till it is translucent. Add the chopped pepper or tomatoes and the grain. Stir well to incorporate the butter. Add water, salt and pepper, cover and simmer for 20 minutes. It may need more water and further simmering. It should be tender yet dry, but is still good rather wet—better that way than gritty, so don't worry about overcooking as much as you would with rice.

For a filling main course, serve on its own with grated cheese or a lentil dish.

Rice

Recipe books are full of detailed and earnest accounts of how to cook perfect rice. Even reading them makes me tired. Below is my sloppy method of cooking rice. It works more than half the time.

I usually use organically grown long-grain brown rice, which is good-natured and tasty. If you want a white rice, basmati is not too temperamental either, and has a distinctive dry smell and taste.

Steamed Rice

> 12 oz (350 g) rice
> 2¼ times its volume of water
> 1 teaspoon salt if you like it

Bring everything to a fast boil, turn down the heat as low as possible, and cook covered till the water is absorbed and the grains just tender. This takes about 10 minutes for white rice and 25–45 for brown (with brown rice, a lot depends on how old the rice is, but old age will not make it inedible unless your kitchen storage area is humid or weevilly).

Once the rice is cooked, it is best if you put a folded tea-towel under the lid and leave it to sit in a warm place for 5 minutes or till you want to serve it, but you can use it at once.

Variations on plain rice

If you are following a risotto or pilaff recipe but using brown rice, *don't* cook it in the fat before adding water, even if you are directed to. This treatment hardens whole rice grain, so that it can take some bits well over an hour to soften, by which time other bits will be mushy. Cook the rice first by the method above, but take it off the heat just short of tender enough. Fry other listed ingredients, mix into the rice, and replace on a very low heat for 10 minutes to let the flavours mingle.

Two very simple variations on plain rice are rice with green herbs and rice with whole spices.

For herbs, add a teacupful of chopped fresh herbs and 2 oz (50 g) butter or 2 tablespoons of olive oil to the basic recipe.

For spices, add 4 cloves, 1-inch (2.5 cm) stick of cinnamon, 4 crushed cardamoms and a broken bay leaf, fried in 2 oz (50 g) butter.

In either case, mix the garnish into the just-cooked rice, replace the lid, and leave to stand for 5 minutes.

Vegetables

The counsel of perfection is to steam vegetables briefly and serve them plain. Wonderful—if your vegetables are tender, pristine fresh, unbloated by excess watering, and unflavoured by the swimming-pool of chlorine some nations dunk them in to rid them of bacteria. The Israelis are particularly keen on this type of purification, though I can find no reference to it in Deuteronomy. The Californians prefer a squirt of perfumed air-freshener, or is it deodorant? The South Africans seem to have confidence in their own cleanliness and don't take precautions of this sort—such a pity they're ideologically unsound: still, one better than the Chileans, whose carrots are slimy as well as fascist by the time they reach the Outer Hebrides. And now the English turnips are going to be irradiated so that the poor Scots won't know they've been out of the ground for 2 years.

You will guess from the above that my vegetable store is multinational and I am seldom in a position to serve the plain steamed perfection, at least before July when our own start growing.

Tolerable vegetables can be successfully treated, after steaming or boiling, with white sauce. Use part milk, part cooking water in the sauce, and flavour with nutmeg, cheese or parsley. Another possibility is a purée, which is especially good for a combination of root vegetables—carrot and parsnip, swede and potato. Don't believe any book which tells you to make purées ahead and heat them up later. Once the vegetable is crushed it immediately starts to oxidise, and your delicately flavoured and tinted masterpiece will taste like hospital 2 veg. if you don't serve it pretty immediately. Purées need lots of butter or cream to make them nice, but if you keep quiet you will find that calorie-conscious ladies who would regard chips as indecent proposals will lap them up: they look so very pretty and dainty.

The following recipes will restore a semblance of health to vegetables past their prime, or to overwatered imports.

Sesame Aubergines

Use only a little oil at a time to fry aubergines—otherwise you will find the whole bottle has gone, with consequent harm to your digestion.

These also make a nice first course, sprinkled with lemon juice.

> 2 large aubergines
> salt
> 2–3 oz (50–75 g) sesame seeds
> ¼ pt (150 ml) sunflower or corn oil

Remove the tops from the aubergines and cut them into thin lengthwise slices. Salt them and leave in a colander for 45 minutes. Rinse them and drain them but don't dry.

Put the sesame seeds on a plate. Press the aubergine slices into them and fry in hot oil. Be careful—the seeds burn easily. Serve at once —they wilt.

Casserole of Aubergine and Potato

> 1 large aubergine
> its weight in potatoes
> 1 medium onion
> 1 red pepper
> ½ lb (225 g) tomatoes
> 2 cloves garlic
> 3 tablespoons olive oil
> juice of 1 lemon

Cut the aubergine into 1-inch (2.5 cm) chunks, salt, and leave to drain in a colander for 45 minutes. Scrub or peel the potatoes and slice. Slice the onion and pepper thinly. Crush the garlic with salt. Skin and seed the tomatoes if you prefer to, but strain and keep the juice from the seeds. Squeeze the lemon.

Get the oil hot in a deep pan. Put in the onion and pepper and cook for 1 minute, stirring once or twice. Add the potatoes, garlic, tomatoes and lemon juice. Wash and dry the aubergine chunks, and mix them in. Simmer for 15 minutes and test for salt. The aubergines may have retained enough. Simmer till the potatoes are just cooked. If there is a lot of juice, cook uncovered on a high heat for a minute or so to reduce it. The finished dish should have sheen and coherence.

Lemon Cabbage

This is about the best you can do with these sinister luminescent footballs which infest Scottish greengrocers for 9 months of the year.

1½ lb (675 g) white cabbage
1 teaspoon caraway seeds
juice of 1 lemon
¼ pt (150 ml) water
salt
a knob of butter

Shred the cabbage finely and put it in a pan with the other ingredients. Cover and cook very fast for 3 minutes. If the cabbage is still tough for your liking, cook a bit longer, but watch for drying out.

Carrot and Potato Cake

This is light and colourful, particularly good with fish.

1 medium onion
2 oz (50 g) butter
½ lb (225 g) carrots
1 lb (450 g) potatoes
½ teaspoon salt

Butter an 8-inch (20 cm) sandwich tin thickly. Chop the onion finely and sauté in the rest of the butter till golden.

Scrub or peel the carrots and potatoes. Grate the carrots and mix into the onion with the salt. Slice the potatoes thinly.

Spread half the carrot mixture in the bottom of the tin. Cover with the sliced potatoes and top with the rest of the carrot. Put a round of greaseproof or Bakewell paper on top and press down.

Cook in a moderate oven for about 25 minutes, till a knife goes easily through the centre. When you take the tin out, press the contents down again and leave for a minute or so before turning out.

Julienne of Celery and Potato

This one is good with game.

1 small onion
1 oz (25 g) butter
1 lb (450 g) potatoes
1 head celery
salt

Chop the onion finely and sauté it gently in the butter. Peel the potatoes and cut them into strips like thin chips. (If this is too fiddly, cut them into thin slices.) Add to the onion.

Clean the celery and cut across or transversely in narrow slices. Add it to the other vegetables with a little salt and fry uncovered, stirring occasionally, for 5 minutes. Now cover the pan and cook on a very low heat till the potato is just tender, but not mushy.

This is rather pallid, though delicious, so use plenty of parsley to garnish.

Courgettes with Tomato Sauce

1½ lb (675 g) courgettes
For the sauce:
1 small onion
1 tablespoon olive oil
1 lb (450 g) tomatoes
2 teaspoons tomato purée
marjoram or oregano to taste
salt and a pinch of sugar
a blade of mace or a scrape of
    nutmeg

For the sauce:

Chop the onion and sauté it in the oil till soft. Slice the tomatoes and add with all the other ingredients. Simmer for 5 minutes. If it is watery, add another teaspoon of tomato purée and boil fast for 2 minutes. Liquidise and strain the sauce and reheat.

Meanwhile, cut the courgettes in rings or diagonal slices ¼-inch (6 mm) thick. Steam them, or fry in a little oil, till just tender—they shouldn't be transparent. Dish up and pour the tomato sauce over.

The same sauce is very good with fried aubergine slices. It cuts their greasiness and their sombre colour.

Cucumber with Herbs

I shall never see a cucumber again without thinking of the "repulsant snozzcumbers", "the filthiest-tasting vegetable on earth" consumed in Roald Dahl's *The BFG*. "They is disgusterous! They is sickable! They is rotsome!" laments the eponymous hero of that work. So too are the bent-ended and soft-spotted cucumbers that are often all that is left to me, come Fridays in Spring or Autumn. But with a bit of judicious trimming, they can be rendered edible by the following treatment.

2 cucumbers
a pinch of salt
½ oz (15 g) butter
a teacup of mixed herbs—parsley,
    chives, and mint or dill

Cut the cucumbers, unpeeled, into small chunks. To do this quickly, slit them lengthwise. Lay each half face down, side by side, slit again twice each, then cut across all the strips at ½-inch (1.25 cm) intervals.

Put the cucumber in a pan with the butter and salt in the bottom and scatter on ¾ of the herbs. Cover and cook fairly fast for 4–5 minutes. Drain and serve garnished with the remaining herbs.

This is disgusterous tepid and rotsome kept hot, but eaten at once it is scrumdiddlyumptious.

Fennel with Tomatoes

1 medium onion
1 tablespoon olive oil
1 lb (450 g) fennel
1 red pepper
1 lb (450 g) tomatoes
a little basil or tarragon
salt and pepper

Chop the onion and sauté in the oil till transparent. Slice the fennel and pepper and add to the onion. Skin the tomatoes, seed them, and retain the juice from the seeds. Crush the garlic with the salt, and add it and the other seasonings. Simmer for 10–15 minutes. If it is too liquid, boil hard for another minute or so.

This is a very pleasant sauce with plain pasta.

Gratin of Fennel

This is good enough to be served as a starter, in which case use a thicker topping of crumbs and cheese.

For the fennel:
2 lb (900 g) fennel
juice of 1 lemon
½ oz (15 g) butter
3 tablespoons water
a little salt
For the sauce:
1½ oz (40 g) butter
1½ oz (40 g) flour
½–¾ pt (275–425 ml) milk
chopped fennel tops
1 tablespoon cream (optional)
For the topping:
1 oz (25 g) grated cheese
½ oz (15 g) brown breadcrumbs

For the fennel:
   Trim the bulbs, reserving the better bits of green. Slice them from top to bottom, and then across in thin strips. Put in a shallow pan with the other ingredients, and simmer till tender—about 7 minutes. Drain, keeping the juice.
For the sauce:
   Melt the butter and add the flour, and when it turns pale, pour on the fennel juices and gradually add the milk. It should be thickish but still pouring. Simmer for 1 minute, add the fennel tops, and test for salt. You can add a tablespoon of cream if you want.
   Put the fennel in an ovenproof dish. Pour over the sauce, and scatter the cheese and breadcrumbs on top. Bake near the top of a hot oven for 10 minutes or till the top browns and crisps.

Sweet and Sour Leeks

Leeks done like this are very good with fish and shellfish, and also on their own with a rice dish. The colour is strange, so have a bright garnish ready—lemon slices or parsley.

approximately 1-inch (2.5 cm)
   cube of tamarind pulp
¼ pt (150 ml) boiling water
6 medium leeks
1 dessertspoon sunflower oil
1–2 teaspoons brown sugar
salt

Soak the tamarind in the hot water for at least 15 minutes. Trim the leeks but keep as much green as possible. Cut them in narrow rings and dabble them in cold water to get out the grit. Drain them well.

Heat the oil and turn the leeks in it till well coated. Add the sugar and salt. Squash the tamarind in your fingers to liberate its sour juice. Press this liquor through a sieve and pour onto the leeks. Mix well, cover, and simmer for 5 minutes. Take off the lid, raise the heat, and boil till the liquid reduces to almost nothing.

Casserole of Sweet Peppers

This looks best made with mixed coloured peppers—red, green and yellow. If all green, the result is slightly bitter as well as dingy in colour. If all red peppers are used, it goes particularly well with fish or pasta.

1 tablespoon olive oil
1 medium onion
6 peppers
1 lb (450 g) tomatoes
salt, sugar and black pepper to
   taste

Chop the onion and sauté in the olive oil. Cut the peppers into ½-inch (1.25 cm) strips and add them too.

Skin and seed the tomatoes, draining the juice from the seeds. Add tomatoes and juice and the seasonings. Mix well, cover and cook slowly for 20 minutes.

If a lot of juice has formed, ladle it into a frying pan and boil it hard to reduce to a couple of tablespoons. Pour it back over the peppers. Don't boil the peppers themselves hard to reduce the liquid, as they will mush up and the skin will separate and toughen.

Potatoes

The next three recipes are for potatoes. I could have made it thirty rather than three: I love potatoes in any form, though I would stop short of the rotten ones mixed with grass, as recommended to the starving Irish by an English peer, during the blight of 1845.

Not everyone is enamoured of even the wholesome tuber: when the Macneill of Barra ordered his people to plant potatoes rather than grain so as to have a harvest even in poor weather, they planted them, harvested them, dumped them sullenly at his gate—and starved. Now their descendants plant virtually nothing else.

One of my best potato memories is of earthing up the crop one sunny June, looking straight down the orange throat of a bright-eyed corn-crake, as it craked day-long in a tussock not 10 feet away. Poor corncrakes, they are almost all gone now, prey to feral cats here and God knows what perils in Africa.

My worst potato memory is of sugaring instead of salting them, and not discovering the mistake—no, the worst was miscounting the Château Potatoes so that there were only a total of 3 pea-sized articles left to feed the last table in the dining room. Difficult to choose.

Potatoes in White Wine

I think I borrowed this recipe, more or less, from Anna Thomas's *The Vegetarian Epicure*. I was looking desperately for ways of using up not quite white wine. We had bought several cases of indifferent Soave at the end of a season, and by next April it was turning ominously amber and beery. Potatoes soak up Soave like sponges. This was a wonderful discovery. It tastes very good too.

1 oz (25 g) butter	salt and pepper
1 large onion	3/4 pt (425 ml) white wine
2 lb (900 g) potatoes	chopped parsley
2 bay leaves	

Melt the butter and sauté the sliced onion in it till golden. Meanwhile, scrub or peel the potatoes and cut into large chunks. Add them with all the other ingredients, except the parsley, stirring well. Simmer, covered, till the potatoes are beginning to break up. Stir carefully now and again—don't mush it—and add more wine if it sticks. Garnish with parsley, as the colour is drab.

Skirlie Potatoes

"Skirlie" is a Scottish mixture of fried onions and oatmeal. It is used as a stuffing (see under Roast Pheasant p. 83), as a side dish with mince and boiled potatoes, or as a meal on its own.

Vegetarians can substitute sunflower oil for dripping. As long as you use plenty of onions this tastes fine; but don't use margarine: all the colourants and anti-oxidants will rise up and smite you in this combination.

As an accompaniment, this potato dish is very good with a plain rare roast.

2 lb (900 g) even-sized potatoes
For the skirlie:
1½–2 oz (40–50 g) dripping
1 medium onion

4 oz (100 g) fine or medium
   oatmeal
salt and pepper

Boil potatoes in their skins.
For the skirlie:

Chop the onion fairly finely and fry till just browning. Add the oatmeal, salt and pepper, and continue cooking till it turns pale and then begins to darken. Remove at once from the heat as oatmeal catches easily.

When the potatoes are ready, dish them, cut them into thick slices in the dish, and scatter on the skirlie.

Potatoes with Rosemary

This is very good with lamb and game.

2 tablespoons olive oil
6 × 4-inch (10 cm) sprigs fresh
   rosemary
2 lb (900 g) potatoes (preferably new)
½ clove garlic crushed with a little
   salt

A cast iron casserole is best for this. Heat the oil in it, put in the rosemary, and leave on a very low heat while you scrub the potatoes. Use even-sized small ones or cut large ones into cubes. Dry them and turn them in the oil with the garlic and salt. Cover and cook in a slow oven or on the stove top till tender—about 1 hour. Stir them gently now and again.

Colourful Mixed Salad

The North of Scotland is not good salad country. I use a mixture of anything I can get or grow that tastes or looks fresh.

We get our olive oil (through Yapp's of Mere) from Beaume-de-Venise. It is a lot more drinkable than the sticky wine of the same name, in my opinion.

For the dressing:
½ a small clove of garlic
a pinch of salt
½ teaspoon French mustard
4 tablespoons fruity olive oil
2 tablespoons wine vinegar
For the salad:
1 lettuce
a few spinach leaves
3 sprigs lovage
a small bunch of chives
a sprig of mint
2 tomatoes
½ small red or yellow pepper
2-inch (5 cm) chunk of cucumber
2 stalks of celery
marigold petals, nasturtium heads,
    bergamot, borage or comfrey
    flowers

For the dressing:
Crush the garlic with the salt, add the other ingredients, and whisk or shake. This is enough for 2 or 3 salads.
For the salad:
Wash and dry the lettuce and spinach carefully. Tear it up and put it in a big bowl. Chop the herbs, slice everything else except the flowers and add to the bowl. Sprinkle on the dressing and turn lightly with your hands. Garnish with the chosen flowers—the brighter the better.

Sweets and Puddings

I don't like sweet things much. This was not always so. Leftover pudding used to appeal to me as the main perk of the job; but two or three seasons of dining mainly on meringues and mousses led to a change of heart. For many people, though, the sweet remains the highlight of the meal, so I make conscientious efforts.

As no one is actually hungry by pudding time, the sweet course should always appeal to the eye. I usually have hasty recourse to leaves or flowers, but tastes were not always so simple. Carême, much quoted, referred to "architecture—of which the main branch is confectionery". It was hardly an exaggeration: sweet dishes had for long been a showplace for brilliant technique, fantastic display, and downright vulgarity. In earlier times it had been the custom to move to a specially decorated table or a more elegant room—in extreme cases even to a separate building such as a summerhouse—for the dessert. As if the candied fruit, syllabubs and comfits of this "last remove" were not enough in the way of sticky delights, the tables of the great were decorated throughout the feast with "subtleties", often in sculpted sugar: castles, swans, palaces, knights in armour—in one extreme instance even the Holy Ghost. A picture of Queen Christina of Sweden dining with the Pope, as late as 1668, shows the unfortunate lady seated solitarily, some 20 yards to the right of and 2 yards down from His worldly Holiness, both diners being half concealed behind the turrets and fortifications of a sugar city. Presumably they were not expected to eat them: but who did? Perhaps they were recycled? One hopes they were not fed to the poor or the dogs, to the ruin of their teeth.

Cakes

The first few recipes are not cakes in the tea-time sense, but simply puddings that will sit upright looking pretty on a flat plate.

Almond Cake with Peaches or Pears

To skin peaches or nectarines, try dropping them into boiling water for 20 seconds. It may not work: some varieties have stubborn skins, and even after this treatment the knife will leave them full of nicks, looking as if a mouse has been at them. Cover them with a swirl of cream and no one will ever know.

For the base:
3 oz (75 g) butter
3 oz (75 g) caster or light
  muscovado sugar
3 oz (75 g) ground almonds
1 oz (25 g) plain flour
2 eggs
For the top:
3–4 peaches or pears
1 tablespoon jam or jelly
¼ pt (150 ml) cream
10 almonds

For the base:
Make sure the butter is really soft. Put all the ingredients in a bowl and beat till thoroughly mixed.

Line a 7-inch (17.5 cm) sandwich tin with Bakewell paper and spread the almond mixture in it. Bake in a slow oven till just firm to the touch—about 1 hour. Cool slightly before turning out. It will be moist and fragile, not really spongey.

For the top:
Peel and halve the fruit. Blanch, toast and chop the almonds. Whip the cream till stiff.

Spread the cake with the jam or jelly—plum, apricot or quince are the best choices. Arrange the fruit round the base. Pipe the cream in swirls over the fruit and scatter on the toasted almonds.

Blackcurrant and Cinnamon Tart

This is my slapdash version of the French Tarte Canelle.
If you have any pastry left make it into biscuits.

> *For the pastry:*
> 6 oz (175 g) plain flour
> 1 level tablespoon ground
>   cinnamon
> 3 oz (75 g) caster sugar
> 3 oz (75 g) butter
> 2 egg yolks or 1 whole egg
> *For the filling:*
> 1 lb (450 g) blackcurrants
> 4 oz (100 g) light muscovado sugar
> 2 teaspoons arrowroot

Rub the butter into the flour, cinnamon and sugar till it begins to stick like shortbread. Bind with the egg. If you use whole egg the pastry will be slightly harder. Let the pastry rest while you pick over the blackcurrants. Remove gross débris but don't worry about the odd unripe berry or the tufty bits at the end. Put the currants in a pan with the sugar over a moderate heat, till the juice runs and boils up. Simmer for 2 or 3 minutes and test to see if they need more sugar, but don't oversweeten.

Cool 2 tablespoons of the juice slightly in a cup and add the arrowroot to it. Mix till smooth, pour into the currants, and bring back to the boil, stirring. As soon as the juice thickens, take off the heat and cool.

You can use a tin of blackcurrants, failing fresh—just thicken the strained juice with the arrowroot and return the currants to it.

Roll out the pastry fairly thick and line a 7–8 inch (17.5–20 cm) flan ring. Bake blind—about 30 minutes in a moderate oven. Watch it—it burns easily.

Cool the pastry shell before removing the ring. If it looks like breaking, leave the ring on.

Pour the filling in. Don't chill: this is best at room temperature.

Serve cream separately, if at all, as it doesn't improve the appearance and not everyone likes the way it blunts the intense flavour of black fruit.

Chilled Cheesecake

This is the first recipe I ever wrote down, 20 years ago when cheese-cakes were still considered rather daring in Scotland. It is a great favourite, though far from original: I got it from a school friend's mother who I think found it in *Good Housekeeping*, so I don't know who to thank for it.

I never get it ready in time to chill thoroughly, so it usually collapses, but if you can give it a couple of hours in the fridge, it will turn out beautifully, firm yet creamy.

For the top:
3 eggs
4 oz (100 g) caster sugar
¼ pt (150 ml) double cream
12–14 oz (350–400 g) curd cheese
   (I use yoghurt cheese)
grated rind and juice of 2 large
   lemons
½ oz (15 g) gelatine
For the base:
8 digestive biscuits
1 oz (25 g) Demerara sugar
1 oz butter

For the top:
Line the base of an 8-inch (20 cm) cake tin.

Separate the eggs. Whisk the yolks with the sugar and lemon rind till thick and light. Do this over a pan of steaming (not boiling) water if you are not using an electric mixer, to speed things up.

Melt the gelatine in the lemon juice and blend with the yolk mixture. Don't have the mixture cooler than room temperature or the gelatine will form strings.

Half whip the cream and mix it into the curd cheese. Add this to the first bowl.

Whisk the egg whites till very stiff and fold them in lightly. Turn the mixture gently into the prepared tin.

For the base:
Crush the digestive biscuits and mix in the sugar. Add the melted butter and sprinkle the buttery crumbs evenly on the cake. Press down lightly and chill, overnight if possible, then turn out and decorate—you can use cream, fresh soft fruit, grated chocolate or green leaves.

Chestnut Cake with Apricot Sauce

When turned out, this pudding bears a superficial resemblance to a block of choc ice at a kids' party, but beware! It is extremely solid and should be served in thin slices. The greedy may well wish to come back for more.

For the cake:
4 oz (100 g) butter
3 oz (75 g) dark muscovado sugar
1 tin unsweetened chestnut purée
2 oz (5 oz) cocoa
1 oz (25 g) white sugar
3 tablespoons water
½ teaspoon vanilla essence
For the sauce:
4 oz (100 g) sour dried apricots
½ pt (275 ml) water or a little less
honey
apricot brandy
For decoration:
¼ pt (150 ml) cream (optional)

For the cake:
Beat the butter and muscovado sugar together in a cursory way. Turn the chestnut purée out of the tin and mash it well. Mix it with the butter and sugar.

Mix the cocoa, white sugar and water to a paste and simmer for 2 minutes. Cool slightly, but while still warm add to the chestnut mixture. Add the vanilla essence and beat everything hard together —the warmth of the sauce will help to make everything blend.

Line a loaf tin with foil or Bakewell paper and pour in the chestnut mixture. Chill well.

For the sauce:
Stew the apricots in the water till soft. Liquidise, with the juice. Sweeten to taste with honey and apricot brandy.

To serve:
Turn out the cake on a plate. Either pour over a little of the sauce just before serving and pass round the rest, or decorate with cream and hand the sauce separately.

Chocolate Chestnut Cake

Chestnuts are not everyone's cup of nut. My father was a doctor, and every Christmas he got about a hundredweight of assorted chocolates and candies from grateful patients, which kept us all munching till spring. In the early sixties, to everyone's disgust, a new confectionery fashion entered middle class life—marrons glacés. Box after box poured in, and piled up, despised, in a corner of the hall cupboard. About the end of February, having run out of chocolates, I discovered I liked them. Then I discovered I liked them better with cream. The pile of marrons grew smaller and I grew larger. At school I read of a similar grossness which afflicted the Mossynoeci, "flabby and very white, fattened up by feeding on boiled chestnuts", according to Xenophon.

Theirs were not even boiled with sugar, let alone served with cream. This cake has both of those and chocolate too. I invented it to use up sweetened chestnut purée bought in error—what else can you do with the stuff?

    8 oz (225 g) dark chocolate
    ¼ pt (150 ml) water
    1 tin sweetened chestnut purée
    3 eggs.
    2 oz (50 g) sugar
    ½–¾ pt (275–425 ml) double
        cream

Melt the chocolate in the water over gentle heat. Separate the eggs. Whisk the yolks with the sugar till thick and pale.

Blend half the chocolate into the chestnut purée till smooth. If you haven't a food processor, it may help to put the purée through a mouli or sieve first.

Fold the chestnut mixture gently into the whisked yolks and sugar. Whip the egg whites stiffly and fold them in too.

Put discs of Bakewell paper in the bottoms of 3 7-inch (17.5 cm) sandwich tins and divide the mixture between them. Bake in a very moderate oven until just firm—about 40 minutes. Leave in the tins to cool. The cake will sink, but remain light and moist.

For the filling:

Cool the rest of the chocolate mixture, whip the cream stiffly, and combine, leaving slightly marbled. Use this to sandwich and coat the cake.

Hazelnut Meringue Cake

"Tell me, how do you get the skins off your hazelnuts?" a knowledge-able guest once asked me.

I was very embarrassed. It had never occurred to me to skin hazelnuts. When she explained how she toasted hers in the oven and rubbed them in a rough cloth, I realised why hazelnut meringue in smart places is rather dry and brown. I prefer it like this—moist, slightly gooey, with untidy nibs of nut in it. But if you want to do things properly, toast and rub them, then grind very finely.

For the meringue:
4 oz (100 g) hazelnuts
4 egg whites
9 oz (250 g) caster sugar
1 teaspoon vinegar
½ teaspoon vanilla essence

For the filling:
½–¾ pt (275–425 ml) double cream
3 peaches *or* ¾ lb (350 g) raspberries *or* 4 oz (100 g) strong chocolate melted in 3 tablespoons water

Grind the hazelnuts. Whisk the egg whites very stiff. Add the sugar, vinegar and vanilla essence, and whisk again till glossy—not too long or it will liquefy. Fold in the nuts.

Divide the mixture between 3 sandwich tins with lined bases—I use a 6-inch (15 cm), a 7-inch (17.5 cm) and an 8-inch (20 cm) tin and make a volcano-shaped cake, but 3 7-inch (17.5 cm) tins are fine.

Bake in a very moderate oven till pale brown and crisp—about 45 minutes. To loosen, run a knife round the edge of the pans. Turn out and peel off the papers before they are completely cold, or they may stick.

For the filling:

Whip the cream stiffly. If you are using chocolate, have it melted and cool and add it to ⅔ of the cream. Use this to layer the cakes and spread the top, and decorate with the plain cream. You can add nuts and grated chocolate.

If you are using fruit, peel and slice the peaches, saving an unsliced half till it is time to decorate as peaches go brown quickly; or pick over the raspberries, keeping back the best berries for the top. Use half the cream for the layers, and the rest of the fruit. Decorate the top with the remaining cream, adding the reserved fruit at the last minute.

You can use tinned raspberries, but drain them very well. Use some of the juice to tint the cream for the top.

A combination of chocolate *and* fruit is very good.

Any meringue is best filled 2 or 3 hours ahead, but I don't like it left longer, as it loses all its texture.

Meringues

Meringue desserts are well liked, and they are about the only useful way of using up egg whites—unless someone has mistakenly drunk weedkiller on your premises: take the egg whites raw for that.

A lot of cooks find problems with meringue making. Take my husband for example. One day I left him with 4 egg whites, a bag of sugar, a whisk and an oven set at 100°C/200°F. "Can you make meringues?" I asked, and rushed out. Some hours later, I got back and looked in the oven, where a dozen or so pallid biscuit-shaped objects were deliquescing ominously.

"I thought they would rise," he said, feebly.

Here are a few hints for meringue making:

(1) Have everything as dry as possible. Even a damp day or a steamy kitchen can cause ooziness or sticking.

(2) Use *fresh* eggs, don't get more than a spot of yolk in the white, and whisk only when you are ready to bake; all these things will affect the amount of air you can incorporate.

(3) Use Bakewell paper for lining if you can get it.

(4) Don't have too high a heat—the meringue will swell, crack and ooze. It will taste lovely, but stick like superglue.

(5) If you do end up with paper firmly stuck to your meringue, turn it over on the tray. Wring out a cloth in warm water and leave it pressed to the paper for 10 minutes. The paper should then lift with the help of a knife. If it doesn't, repeat the process till it does.

(6) If nothing works and you end up with smashed and sticky remnants, don't despair. Mix them lightly with whipped cream, flavoured if you like with chocolate, vanilla or a liqueur, and layer with fruit or toasted almonds. See the recipe for Summer Trifle (p. 120) for an example.

The basic meringue mixture is as follows:

4 egg whites
8 oz (225 g) caster sugar

Whisk the egg whites till very stiff, but still slightly shiny. Add 1 oz (25 g) of the sugar and whisk again. Fold in the rest of the sugar with a metal spoon or a spatula and bake at once.

Have tins lined before you start with Bakewell paper or 2 layers of greased greaseproof paper or foil. Bake in a low oven until crisp and dry—2 hours minimum.

For ordinary meringues, make 16 even-sized blobs. When cold, sandwich with cream and decorate with a glacé cherry and a bit of angelica if you like vulgar bright colours, as I do.

For a meringue cake, make 4 small or 3 larger flat rounds. When cool, sandwich and spread them with cream or buttercream flavoured with chocolate and coffee—6 oz (175 g) chocolate and 2 teaspoons instant coffee melted in 5 tablespoons water, added when cool to ½ pt (275 ml) whipped cream. You can call this Gâteau Diane, though it isn't quite.

Alternatively, sandwich with cream and fresh fruit, and decorate imaginatively with swirls of cream, some strawberries, flowers or leaves. This is also not quite, but call it a Vacherin. It's as good as.

Things in Bowls

If you have a nice cut glass or glazed bowl, you needn't fear failures with sweets. Fallen cakes, broken meringues, collapsed moulds and liquid creams can all be made to look tolerable in a pretty container, with the addition of whipped cream, fruit or nuts. The recipes below, though, I have actually evolved with cut glass in mind, rather than as rescue operations.

Several of these recipes call for gelatine. To get an even, light texture without strings, timing and temperature are both important. The egg yolk mixture must not be too cold, or the gelatine will form hard lumps as soon as it touches it. Once the gelatine is incorporated, keep an eye on it, as it may set very quickly: fresh lemon juice in particular can have that effect. You can put the bowl into cold water to start it setting, but don't forget it. The cream (if any) should go in just as the yolk mixture starts to thicken. Don't try to cut work by whisking egg whites in advance: they will begin to lose their airiness at once. And above all, don't use the sort of egg that says Week 42 on the packet when you are living in Week 48. Warmish gelatine is an ideal growing medium for all sorts of bugs, and all sorts of bugs thrive in ancient battery eggs.

Strict vegetarians may baulk at gelatine, as it is made from boiled sinews. Agar-agar is a substitute, but you only need ¼ as much, and it has to be boiled in some of the liquid from the recipe till it gels. The caramel mousse in this section will stiffen reasonably without any gelling agent at all.

Caramel Mousse

Caramel is very easy once you are used to it, but be prepared for blackness and the fumes of Hell if you haven't tried it before.

Be careful when handling a pan of hot caramel. Always wrap a teatowel round the hand holding the pan, and if you have to add water tilt the pan away from you and hold it under a drizzling tap, unless you are incapable of judging quantities. If you have to use a measuring jug, cover the hand holding that as well.

In this recipe, more yolks than whites will give a creamier, closer texture, but I prefer the lighter effect of equal proportion. Like all caramel sweets, this is very good with fresh fruit, especially oranges.

3 eggs, or 4 yolks and 2 whites
1 tablespoon water
8 oz (225 g) granulated sugar
¼ pt (150 ml) water
1½ teaspoons gelatine melted in
  2 tablespoons water
½ pt (275 ml) double cream

Beat the egg yolks till thick and pale.

Dissolve the sugar slowly in the tablespoonful of water over gentle heat, and when it is clear, raise the heat as high as possible. Have ready a drizzling tap or ¼ pt (150 ml) water in a jug, and a covering for your hand. Put a little cold water in the sink.

When the syrup has gone from gold to amber to a rich russet brown, take the pan quickly and dip the bottom of it in the water in the sink. Trickle in the ¼ pt (150 ml) water, and when the explosions subside, put the pan back on the heat briefly and stir till the caramel is dissolved.

Cool the caramel for 5 minutes. Meanwhile dissolve the gelatine and whip the cream, but not the egg whites yet.

Pour the caramel onto the egg yolks. If you are using an electric beater do this while the whisk is turning at high speed: otherwise whisk like mad immediately afterwards, in case the caramel sets stickily in the bottom of the bowl. Whisk till pale and thick again. Stir in the gelatine, and cool the mixture. It will set before it is really cold, so when it is tepid, whisk the egg whites stiff. Fold in half the cream, followed by the egg whites, and turn into a serving bowl. Decorate with the rest of the cream.

Once you are confident with caramel, you can set some of it hard for decoration. To do this, oil a small baking tin. When the caramel is brown, dip the pan in the sink as directed to stop it darkening any further, and pour a thin layer of it into the tin before adding the water. When this sets, break or crush it and scatter it on top of the mousse. Caramel absorbs moisture quickly, so don't put it on till you are almost ready to serve, or it will sweat.

For the same reason, some good news. If you stick up your pans with unsuccessful caramel, they will usually wash clean after a soaking, unless utterly carbonised.

Cold Orange Soufflé

3 eggs
2 oz (50 g) caster sugar
grated rind of 2 oranges
juice of 3 oranges
juice of 1 lemon
2 teaspoons gelatine
¼ pt (150 ml) double cream
For decoration:
12 walnut halves
1 tablespoon caster sugar

Separate the eggs. Whisk the yolks till thick with the sugar and orange rind. Dissolve and melt the gelatine in 4 tablespoons of the orange juice.

Add the rest of the juices to the cream and whip till it holds a peak. Stir the gelatine into the egg yolks. Don't have the yolks too cold or it will string.

As soon as the mixture starts setting, fold in the cream. Whisk the egg whites stiffly and fold them in too. Turn into a bowl.

For decoration:

Put the walnuts and sugar in a small heavy pan on a medium heat till the sugar melts, then turn up the heat till the mixture browns and bubbles. Have ready an oiled baking tin, pour the caramelised walnuts onto this and push apart quickly with a metal fork. Just before serving, place them on the mousse.

If you don't fancy caramelising, decorate with grated chocolate or fresh orange segments.

Frangipane Cream with Plum Compôte

The texture of this cream bears an unfortunate resemblance to cold semolina pud, but the taste is very delicate and distinctive. It goes well with a compôte of red plums.

On the subject of red plums, I once had a tray of them in the shed where I keep the fruit and vegetables. One night they disappeared. The box was there, but the plums were not. Everything else was as before. The following day I reached into the paper sack of carrots—and reached—and reached—no carrots either! We were mystified. Neighbours' boys playing practical jokes? Light-fingered campers? We rigged up a makeshift burglar alarm against further raids, but nothing else happened. We looked askance at the suspected campers, and grumbled.

A couple of weeks later, we smelt a rat—a dead one. We moved everything in our search, including the pallets on which the fruit boxes stood. We didn't find the rat but we found his treasures, now much decayed—40 red plums and 30 carrots: not even nibbled, but stored up in red and orange glory for him to gloat over. Vanity, vanity! It was so pathetic I cried. We bought a humane rat trap and baited it with Stilton to catch any other marauders. The Stilton was appreciated. In the course of a fortnight our visitor ate about a pound of prime Stilton, rejecting dried-up cheddar crusts. But he always left before we got up in the morning. Late one night we crept in and caught him at dinner. We took him to the local rubbish dump to try his fortunes there. I hope the local gang didn't scrag him.

For the Cream:
3 egg yolks
3 oz (75 g) sugar
¾ pt (425 ml) milk
2 teaspoons gelatine melted in
   2 tablespoons water
finely grated rind of 1 orange
3 drops almond essence
1 tablespoon orange flower water
   (if it's the concentrate, use only
   3 drops)
2 oz (50 g) ground almonds
¼ pt (150 ml) double cream
10 split toasted almonds

For the Compôte:
1½ lb (675 g) red or black plums
¼ lb (100 g) light muscovado sugar
2-inch (5 cm) strip orange peel
2 cloves
1 glass port or red wine

For the Cream:

Blend the egg yolks with the sugar. Boil the milk, pour it on to the egg yolks, stirring all the time, and return the mixture to the pan. Cook very slowly till it thickens slightly but do not boil, or it will curdle. Pour this custard into a wide bowl. Add the dissolved gelatine, and everything else except the cream. Cool, stirring occasionally, until it begins to set. Whip the cream and fold it in, and turn it into a serving bowl. Decorate with toasted almonds.

For the Compôte:

Stone the plums if you prefer to. Put all the compôte ingredients in a pan and let the contents boil up once. Reduce heat to very low and barely simmer till the plums are just soft. Add more sugar if necessary, but don't lose the slightly bitter plum taste by oversweetening. Chill before serving.

Rose Cream

This recipe is plagiarised from Damask Cream in Theodora Fitzgibbon's *A Taste of the West Country*. I make it less creamy. It is very simple and unusual.

> *For the junket:*
> 1½ pt (825 ml) milk
> 2 oz (50 g) caster sugar
> 1 tablespoon rosewater
> a drop of red colouring
> 1 teaspoon essence of rennet
> nutmeg
> *For the top:*
> ¼ pt (150 ml) double cream
> 1 tablespoon rosewater
> red rose petals

For the junket:

Warm the milk and sugar to blood heat. Add the rosewater, colouring and rennet. Stir well, and pour into a glass bowl or 6 individual ones. Set in a warm place without moving until firm. Grate nutmeg over fairly liberally. Cool.

For the top:

Half-whip the cream and rosewater and pour it over the junket. Chill. Scatter rose petals on just before serving.

Summer Trifle

This is best if you make your own sponge cake and use it very fresh, but you can substitute bought sponge fingers. The lack of custard and the addition of egg white to the whipped cream make it lighter and fresher than a Christmassy trifle

Actually the kind of trifle I like best is the solid institutional sort, with bloated sponge cake suspended in red jelly of the consistency of gristle, topped by 2 yellow inches of unyielding custard, if possible made with dried milk powder. But the honest old school-party trifle is hard to find these days; its sophisticated descendant is beautified with sweet and slimy preparations of sodium alginate, Saccharin and citric acid—no-cook custard, instant jelly and sort of shaving foam on top. Only the hundreds and thousands are what they always were, and they were the only bit I didn't like.

For the sponge cake:
2 eggs
2 oz (50 g) caster sugar
2 oz (50 g) plain flour
For the filling:
4 tablespoons apricot brandy or
    strawberry or raspberry liqueur
2–3 peaches or nectarines
½ lb (225 g) strawberries
For the top:
½ pt (275 ml) double cream
1 egg white
1 pt (570 ml) volume broken
    meringues or ½ pt (275 ml)
    macaroons

For the sponge:
Preheat the oven to 200°C/400°F. Grease an 8-inch (20 cm) sandwich tin and line the base. Whisk the eggs and sugar till very light and thick. Fold in the flour gently and turn into the tin. Bake till just firm—about 8 minutes.
For the filling:
Peel the peaches and slice all the fruit, but save the best few strawberries for the top. Pour the liqueur over the sliced fruit.
Line a bowl with the cut up sponge cake and put the fruit on top.

For the top:
Whisk the cream and egg white separately till fairly stiff and combine gently. Fold in the meringues or macaroons, not crushed but in rough pieces. Pile this onto the fruit and decorate with the reserved strawberries. Chill for an hour, when the meringue will have begun to melt pleasantly.

Syllabub

This recipe also makes a refreshing ice cream to serve with peaches or melon. If you freeze it, take it out and mash it a couple of times or it will separate.

    juice of 2 lemons
    ¼ pt (150 ml) white wine, dry or
        sweet
    caster sugar to taste—1–3 oz
        (25–75 g)
    ½ pt (275 ml) double cream
    nutmeg or cinnamon

Whisk the cream with the sugar till fairly thick. Add the juice and wine in 2 or 3 instalments, whisking between additions to a soft peak. Taste for sweetening. If the cream looks as if it will take it without curdling, add a little extra wine. Turn into a glass bowl or 6 long-stemmed glasses, and sprinkle the chosen spice over.
You can serve brandy snaps, macaroons or fresh fruit with this.

Ices

I am not going to describe the correct procedures for making various sorts of ices. They are fiddly and tiresome like many correct procedures, and you can make ices of character without knowing anything about them. The following are all personal experiments. Do try your own—you can use anything from avocadoes to evaporated milk with cocoa.
To freeze, preferably use a flat-bottomed metal container on the bottom of the freezing compartment—not on top of other packages.

Butterscotch Ice Cream

This is quite a lot of bother but extremely good.

8 oz (225 g) dark muscovado sugar	a further 2 tablespoons water
4 oz (100 g) butter	3 eggs
⅛ pt (75 ml) water	¼ pt (150 ml) double cream
a pinch of salt	*For decoration:*
½ teaspoon vanilla essence	20 toasted almonds

Put the sugar, butter, ⅛ pt (75 ml) water and salt in a heavy pan and boil for 2 minutes on a high heat. It will froth up and then subside, glooping vigorously. (It should be at 110°C/220°F, jam temperature, certainly no hotter.)

Remove it from the heat and add the vanilla and the second dose of water.

Whisk the eggs till pale and thick, and pour in ¾ of the warm butterscotch, beating the while if possible. Continue whisking till it is light and fairly thick again, by which time it should be nearly cool. Whip the cream to a soft peak and fold it into the mixture. Turn into a shallow metal dish and freeze for 2 hours. It is a rich mixture, so it won't go crunchy, but if you don't beat it now and again during freezing, it will separate into a lighter and darker layer. I rather like it that way.

Keep an eye on the rest of the butterscotch, which is for a sauce. If it gets too sticky, heat it up with a little more water and cool again. If it is too runny, heat it to boiling point and stir in 1 level teaspoon arrowroot slaked in 1 tablespoon water.

To serve, pile the ice cream in a serving dish layered with the sauce and toasted almonds.

Milk Ice

This simple recipe comes from my mother-in-law. It's a very light and refreshing ice, but it goes rock hard if kept, so eat it at once—it will be no strain to do so.

I have tried the same method using 1 tablespoon rosewater instead of vanilla, and that is also very good.

1 pt (570 ml) milk	1½ teaspoons gelatine
vanilla essence to taste	3 oz (75 g) sugar

Mix the gelatine and sugar in a pan and add the milk. Heat, stirring, till dissolved. Add vanilla essence to taste (I like it quite strong). Cool, and then freeze. Inspect it every half-hour and mash it a few times after it begins to crystallise.

Cardamom Ice

This and the next two ices are made in the same way. The three together make a sophisticated party sweet. If you plan to do this, make a double or triple quantity of custard, and divide into 3 bowls for flavouring, before adding the egg whites.

  3 eggs
  1 pt (570 ml) milk
  ½ teaspoon agar agar (or
    2 teaspoons gelatine dissolved in
    2 tablespoons water)
  2 oz (50 g) light muscovado sugar
  20 crushed cardamoms

Separate the eggs. Boil the milk with the agar agar (but if you are using gelatine, just melt it and keep it aside). Make a custard with the milk and egg yolks and cook over a very gentle heat till it thickens lightly. Pour it into a wide bowl and add the sugar, and the gelatine if you are using it.

Crush the cardamoms, remove large bits of husk, and add to the custard. Cool the bowl in a sink of cold water, stirring occasionally.

When the custard is cool and beginning to set, fold in the stiffly whisked egg whites. Freeze for 1½ hours, mashing after each half hour.

Cinnamon Ice

Substitute 2–3 teaspoons ground cinnamon for the cardamoms.

Heather Honey Ice

Instead of the sugar, add 2 tablespoons heather honey, and omit the spices.

Hot Puddings

I only use hot puddings on Sundays, as a simple hot English pudding with cream seems a good complement to the Sabbath Lobster Mayonnaise. I often make fruit pies, or if not, one of the following. These are popular with everyone including our dog Jet. Six days a week he sleeps soundly till the main course is served, then stations himself immovably in the breach between kitchen and serving hatch, to intercept tasty morsels on their way to and fro: but he doesn't care for lobster, so on Sundays his pre-prandial slumber is extended till the pudding is broached. His favourite is apple pie (with the cloves removed before he is served) but that is so well known it hardly needs a recipe. Here is his second choice:

Queen of Puddings

½ oz (15 g) butter
1 pt (570 ml) milk
grated rind of 1 lemon
2 oz (50 g) fine breadcrumbs
1 oz (25 g) granulated sugar
2 eggs
½ lb (225 g) home-made jam
4 oz (100 g) caster sugar

Heat the milk with the butter, lemon rind and granulated sugar and pour over the breadcrumbs. Butter a 2-pint (1.2 litre) baking dish. Separate the eggs. Beat the yolks into the bread and milk and pour this custard into the dish. Bake in a very moderate oven till just firm —about 40 minutes. Cool slightly.

Whisk the egg whites very stiffly and fold in the caster sugar. If you happen to have an extra egg white handy, use it, with 2 oz (50 g) more sugar.

Spread the jam on the cooked base. Raspberry jam is traditional, but plum and blackcurrant are very good too: don't use anything too sweet. Pile the meringue on top, sealing the edges, and return to the oven till the top is crisp and brown—about 30 minutes.

Hot Chocolate Pudding

This and the next pudding look rather like failed soufflés—not surprisingly, as they consist of similar ingredients combined in a different manner.

For the sauce:
½ oz (15 g) butter
1 tablespoon golden syrup
1 tablespoon dark muscovado
   sugar
1 tablespoon cocoa

For the top:
½ pt (275 ml) milk
3 oz (75 g) sugar
2 oz (50 g) butter
2 oz (50 g) flour
1 oz (25 g) cocoa
3 eggs

For the sauce:
   Melt all the ingredients together and bring to the boil. Pour into a greased 2-pint (1.2 litre) baking dish.

For the top:
   Whisk the cocoa, sugar and egg yolks together till well mixed. Add the butter cut in small pieces, the flour and milk, and whisk again. Beat the egg whites very stiff and fold gently into the mixture. Pour it over the sauce and bake for 45–50 minutes in a very moderate oven. It should be sticky and dark at the bottom and spongey on top.

Hot Lemon Pudding

4 oz (100 g) sugar
2 oz (50 g) plain flour
1½ oz (40 g) butter
juice and grated rind of 2 lemons
3 eggs
½ pt (275 ml) milk

Separate the eggs and cut the butter into small pieces. Put all the ingredients except the egg whites in a bowl and whisk with a rotary whisk for 1 minute. Whisk the egg whites stiffly and fold in. If you only possess one whisk, make sure it is washed and dried before attacking the egg whites, as any moisture will prevent them fluffing up.

   Fold the egg whites into the mixture and pour into a greased 2-pint (1.2 litre) baking dish. Bake for 45–50 minutes in a very moderate oven.

Bananas Flambées

Andrew claims to have invented this method on a yacht somewhere, but as the recipe he says he used is entirely different except that it contains bananas, either he can't read or he tippled too much of the rum. It is best with a home-made vanilla ice cream, therefore not on a yacht, unless a very advanced one.

6 bananas (underripe work best)
2 oz (50 g) butter
2 oz (50 g) dark muscovado sugar
1 tablespoon raisins
4 tablespoons rum, or more

Slice the bananas in 4 lengthwise and then across once. Melt the butter in a frying pan and put in the bananas. When they turn yellow, add the sugar and the raisins. Turn carefully till everything is hot.

Warm the rum. If you want the bananas in a fancy serving dish get the dish very hot and turn them into it: if it is cool the rum won't blaze. Light the warmed rum and immediately pour over the bananas.

Breakfast

Breakfast has meant different things in different times and places. There is an eighteenth century painting in the Musée Condé entitled "Das Austern Frühstuck"—Austrian breakfast—depicting a company of elegantly dressed young gentlemen starting the day with oysters and champagne. Most of us would not relish oysters for breakfast. The clue to the evident self-satisfaction of this party is perhaps to be found in their activities of the previous night: oysters were much esteemed for aphrodisiac properties, both to stimulate and to restore. The young gallant might down a dozen or so oysters between engagements, as the harassed executive gulps black coffee.

Samuel Johnson was downright in his praise of the Scottish breakfast above all others. "If an epicure could remove by a wish in quest of sensual gratification, wherever he had supped, he would breakfast in Scotland," declared the sage.

I have kind feelings for Dr Johnson because he loved his cat Hodge, and so I am pleased to think that he would have enjoyed our breakfast at Scarista. We start with a cold table of fresh fruit juices, fresh fruit, stewed dried fruit, yoghurt, muesli and other cereals. This is followed by porridge with cream; kippers, bacon, sausages, black, white and raisin-speckled sliced puddings, fried tomatoes, mushrooms, fried bread, eggs; scones, oatcakes, wholemeal toast; and a choice of various coffees and teas.

The vigilant reader (if not bored into quiescence by this catalogue) will have noticed the presence of bacon and sausages. Free range? Yes, of course, though sadly not local. It was a very narrow squeak. When we decided to abandon all factory-farmed produce, bacon was the greatest difficulty. We could ban poultry and pork without anyone really noticing the lack, and augment the deficiencies of our laying hens by applying to a fellow hen-keeper; but bacon seemed impossible. With a week to go before the start of the new season, we gritted our teeth and prepared for ill tempers at baconless breakfasts. Then we heard of Ann Petch in Devon (her address is at the end of this book) who rears rare old breeds of pig and from them produces superb sausages, bacon and hams. A few days after my nervous 'phone call, the first Datapost parcel arrived. Since then all our pigmeat has come in this manner—a special van with a jolly postman on overtime makes the round trip of 110 miles from Stornoway to deliver our sausages. The quality of Mrs Petch's products is unbeatable. The quality of life enjoyed by her pigs looks unbeatable too. We went to see them on our next trip South and shot our whole reel of holiday film on studies of jowly Middle Whites, alert Tamworths, dapper Berkshires and blowsy Gloucester Old Spots. We saw the well-sprung van they go the slaughter house in too, and it looked as stress-free as such a conveyance could be, certainly more comfortable than a Harris bus. Watching Mrs Petch's pigs, I almost felt they had got a decent bargain, and I am not prone to feel that about meat animals.

Fresh Fruit Juices

If you have an electric juice extractor, you can make juice from almost anything, but the only sorts we use are grapefruit and orange. The best method for these is an aluminium hand-juicer. The important thing about fresh fruit juice is that it should be *fresh*. Kept in the fridge overnight, it is hardly distinguishable from the bottled type in taste, and in appearance it is decidedly worse, as the flecks of fruit and the oil from the zest rise to the top.

Dried Fruits

It's a mistake to go straight for the big, brightly coloured moist-looking stuff in sealed packets. Buy your dried fruit from a health food store. Sniff around the sacks and boxes (but surreptitiously, or they may eject you). The best dried fruit has an intense perfume, reminiscent of its fresh sun-warmed self dipped in wine. Don't be put off by small wizened fruits with a powdery white coating: this is just the natural sugar crystallising on the skin. Fruit that is very plump and shiny has been treated with foreign substances (hair oil?) and fruit that is very large was grown in conditions conducive to size and tastelessness: think of Golden Delicious Apples, size 1.

Here are a few types of dried fruit that may be unfamiliar, whose looks alone would not persuade you to buy:

Apricots—Hunza

These are very small whole wild apricots from the Hunza Valley on the borders of Afghanistan. Beautiful must be the mountains whence they come, but you would never guess it to look at these little mud-coloured marbles. Taste them, though, and you will be astonished. They are lusciously sweet, almost buttery. Anyone who has read *The Magician's Nephew* will be reminded of Digory's toffee tree. The kernels are good to eat, too, if you are not inhibited about crunching the stones.

Apricots—Turkish unsulphured

Dried apricots are usually treated with sulphur to retain their colour. These are dark brown, with a rich, warm scent, like heather honey.

Apricots—unprepossessing wizened halves

You sometimes come across small, dry-looking apricots, unevenly coloured from rusty red through orange to greenish yellow. They are usually cheap. Buy them—they are very sour, but have an intense flavour. Use them in savoury dishes, or with other sweeter fruit such as figs, if they are too sharp on their own, or sweeten them cautiously with honey and cinnamon.

Figs—Turkish

The best ones are not over large, but squashy, dark and blooming with crystallising natural sugar. They need very little cooking and are very good without any, instead of sweets.

Prunes—70/80 runts

Prunes are graded by number per kilo. 30/40 are huge and bland, 50/60 are sweet and juicy with a good flavour, and 70/80 are invariably very wrinkled and sour. These smallest cheap ones often have the most pronounced prussic flavour, more than a hint of almonds. As with apricots, use the sourest in savoury dishes, or with a sweeter dried fruit, or add some light muscovado sugar.

I never bother to soak dried fruit. Cover liberally with water, bring to the boil, and simmer very gently till almost tender. The fruit will continue to plump up as it sits in the warm juice. It will keep, covered, for several days.

Fresh Fruit Salad

If you are serving fruit salad for breakfast, it should be sharper and lighter than after a meal, so forget about sugar syrup and liqueurs. I peel apples and peaches for guests, but I prefer them unpeeled personally. If you don't peel, slice finely.

> 1 small melon or pineapple
> 2 apples
> 2 oranges, *or* 1 orange and
>   1 grapefruit
> 2 peaches
> 1 banana
> ¼ lb (100 g) grapes
> juice of ½ lemon

Peel the fruit as necessary and cut into even-sized slices. To get pithless segments out of citrus fruit, peel round and round like an apple and cut out the flesh with a fine saw-bladed knife, leaving the membrane behind. Catch any juice and add with the fruit. Put in the lemon juice, but you may not need it if you used grapefruit.

Muesli

Wholefood muesli mixtures are generally very good these days, but try this for a special occasion. You should use the combination of grains labelled "muesli base" for this. If you can't get hold of it use porridge oats—*not* a sweetened packet muesli. I like the mixture fairly sharp, with yoghurt and no cream, but this depends on individual taste. It is quite tolerable to substitute a mixture of evaporated milk and fruit juice if you have neither cream nor yoghurt, or use all fruit juice. Milk is too bland.

This mixture is quite passable next day, but it is much better eaten at once, when the textures are distinct, with a bit of bite to the grains and dried fruit, and no suggestion of mushiness. It doesn't suit everyone even then—Andrew always refers to it as cold porridge.

> 1 dessertspoon each of:
>   raisins or currants
>   dried apricots
>   shelled but not skinned nuts
> juice of 1 orange and 1 lemon
> 1 dessertspoon of well-flavoured
>   honey
> about a teacupful of sliced fresh
>   fruit
> 1 large tart apple
> 3–4 tablespoons muesli grains
> ¼ pt (150 ml) yoghurt or cream, or
>   rather more

The night before you intend to make the muesli, chop the first three ingredients coarsely together. Stir the honey into the fruit juices and add the chopped mixture and the sliced fresh fruit. Do not peel anything that has edible skin. Chill this mix overnight.

Next morning, grate the whole apple into the bowl, without peeling or coring. Add the muesli grains. Put in enough cream, yoghurt or a mixture of both to make the consistency slightly sloppy—it should *not* resemble porridge.

Taste for sweetness/sharpness. Add more honey, brown sugar or lemon juice, as required.

Garnish with streaks of cream, attractive-looking fruit such as grapes or strawberries, or mint leaves.

Yoghurt

Yoghurt is delicious with stewed dried fruit for breakfast, and has, of course, a multitude of other applications. You can use any sort of milk, pasteurised or not, skimmed or whole, dairy or soya.

Home-made yoghurt is much superior to bought. I used to think patent yoghurt makers were cissy, but after 10 years of struggling to keep batches going in muffled bowls and vacuum flasks, I gave in, and sheepishly bought the cheapest model available at Boots'. Since then I have had consistently perfect yoghurt.

I use a new commercial starter every 6 weeks or so, but skilled hands can keep it going much longer. The first starter I ever battled with was fearsomely rugged. It didn't come in a hygienic bottle or packet—it was fished out of a bubbling bowl of yoghurt by the friend who presented me with it, and looked like a sprig of tough cauliflower. Every evening I offered it a bowl of warm milk, and every morning it had gobbled most of the offering and trebled in size. I drained off whatever it had left (which had turned into a very tangy, effervescing yoghurt) placed the Thing gingerly in a sieve, and washed it ritually three times in running water. Then another libation of milk. By the end of a week it was consuming 2 pints a day and had attained the size of a football. Eventually I plucked up enough courage to put it in the dustbin, but for some time I expected retribution to follow.

Use live yoghurt but not as live as that. Failing instructions with your patent machine, proceed like this:

Have the milk just above blood heat—hot to the touch, but not so hot you can't stick a finger in it. Clean the finger first: warm milk quickly picks up bacteria. If you are using fresh dairy milk, boil it and cool it to the correct temperature; if you have processed milk, heat it. Whisk in 1 teaspoon of live yoghurt, or your starter. Pour into a yoghurt maker, or vacuum flask, or put in a covered bowl in a warm place, insulated with a towel. Investigate at intervals after 3 hours. When the milk thickens, remove it to a cool place. It is best made every day, but will keep up to a week in the fridge.

Porridge

If you use no-cook oats you will end up with wallpaper paste. In fact any sort of rolled oat is just about as bad. Use oatmeal: it comes in pinhead, medium and fine, according to preference. The best porridge I ever ate was my grandmother's, made with fine oatmeal and a lot of salt. She served it in shallow plates. It went satisfyingly solid, so that one could excavate milk rivers and lakes in it. Somehow it was never gelatinous, as mine is if I make it that thick.

In my home area, those over the age of porridge landscaping dunk it spoonful by spoonful in a cup of milk or cream. The top of the porridge is always sprinkled with dry meal, and no one *ever* puts syrup, honey or sugar on it. Indeed, the very thought of this abomination is so disgusting that to this day I can hardly bear to handle the plates where it has been perpetrated.

This quantity is for only 2 servings, as you are unlikely to find many porridge lovers together in time and place.

   3 oz (75 g) oatmeal
   ¾ pt (425 ml) water
   1 flat teaspoon salt

If you are in a hurry in the mornings, soak the meal overnight. Then you need only bring it to the boil, stirring, and it will thicken almost at once. Pinhead meal will need 2 minutes cooking even if it has been soaked, 10 minutes if it hasn't. I use fine with a third of pinhead for texture's sake.

Don't overcook porridge and above all don't let it form a skin. It will develop a steamy flavour like the smell of an old-fashioned wash-day.

Serve liberally sprinkled with dry meal, with milk or cream. Please don't put sugar on it.

Kippers

Bought kippers are scorned by addicts of home smoking, who claim, with justice, that they are insufficiently long in smoke and dyed a silly colour. Nevertheless, if the herring were fresh, even a commercial kipper can be very good. You should never need extra fat to cook a kipper. Heat a dry frying pan, put in the kippers flesh side down, cover with a lid and cook for 2–3 minutes. Turn them over and cook a further minute. You should get about a tablespoonful of evil-looking oil draining from 2 kippers. If you haven't, suspect them of old age. If they make you belch kippery fumes all day, they were certainly past it, or else you are pregnant.

Kedgeree

Kedgeree is a good way of using a small quantity of fish—a couple of smoked whiting or the catch of an unsuccessful fly fisherman. If kept hot it goes very stodgy, so have everything ready, even the previous evening, and just mix at serving time. It will only take 2–3 minutes.

    4 oz (100 g) long grain rice
    4 eggs
    ½–¾ lb (225–350 g) fish
    3 oz (75 g) butter
    salt and freshly ground black
        pepper
    chopped parsley

Cook the rice. Hardboil and chop 3 of the eggs. Cook and flake the fish.

When ready to serve, get the butter very hot in a frying pan. Add first the rice, then the fish, then the eggs, allowing each ingredient to heat through before adding the next. Season to taste. Beat the fourth egg, mix it into the rice, and serve at once, garnished with chopped parsley.

You can make a similar vegetarian dish in exactly the same way, using lightly cooked vegetables instead of fish. Leeks and mushrooms are best. Add some grated nutmeg.

Eggs

Egg production is so fiendishly cruel that I must reiterate its horrors. In a battery cage, a hen has little more room than the page you are reading. To live life-long in such conditions is for her as it would be for you to spend your whole life in your wardrobe, with four other people. Imagine if one of them was a bully, and pulled your hair out, or even bit holes in you. Imagine if the floor of the wardrobe was of wire mesh, and you were barefoot. If that reads like one of Amnesty International's torture files, that is just how it is.

Poached Eggs

To get perfect results, use a rather wide, shallow pan with at least 1½ inches (4 cm) of water in it, over a high heat. Break the first egg into a cup. As soon as the water boils up, slide the egg into it, bringing the cup down to the level of the water. Do the same with the other eggs in quick succession. After the last egg is in, let the water boil up fiercely. Remove from the heat, cover and let stand for 2 minutes. Try to take the eggs out in the order they went in—this is not difficult with up to 4 eggs.

Scrambled Eggs

Scrambling eggs in large quantities is not a success. Allow 1–2 eggs per person depending on what else you are serving. Don't use too much milk (a common practice) or you will get a flavourless curdled custard.

    4 eggs
    1 tablespoon milk
    ¼ flat teaspoon salt
    ½ oz (15 g) butter

Whisk the eggs, milk and salt in a bowl. Melt the butter in a heavy-bottomed pan, pour in the eggs, and stir over a medium heat till you have flakes of egg forming and the rest of creamy consistency. Take off the heat at once, and continue stirring till the flakes predominate. There should still be liquid egg coating them, and it should have a nice satiny sheen. Dish hastily, and eat at once.

As for fried eggs, I can't offer much advice. Frying eggs isn't an area in which I excel. I dislike using a lot of fat, and never believe how much is required to cook an egg. I can't baste them without burning myself, and as I usually cook everything on the highest possible heat, I toughen and brown the undersides. All the same a Scarista fried egg is still a lot better than the recurrent hotel horror of stale battery eggs fried slowly in rancid commercial cooking oil.

Scots turn their eggs—thrifty with fat. When they are almost cooked, flip them over for half a minute before serving. I achieved notoriety at an early age by shouting after an elderly head waiter in a very proper establishment, "I like my egg turned!" A lot of heads turned too. I recollect my parents' faces vividly. My daughter recently avenged them by bellowing in an echoingly empty café in Yorkshire, "*This* isn't real cream!"

Puddings—Maragan

A marag is a pudding—black, white or spotted. They are dearly loved in the Islands. Those we buy and slice for breakfast frying are obtained in plastic skins from Charles Macleod, butchers in Stornoway, who are rightly proud of their puddings. The true traditional marag, though, is made at sheep-killing time, to use up the blood, suet and stomach from the carcase. Some housewives are superb pudding makers, but it is rather a dying art.

Don't be squeamish about these. Better eat the outsides of a sheep one week and the insides the next, than eat the outsides of two and waste the rest.

White Pudding

1 sheep's stomach	6 oz (175 g) suet
¾ lb (350 g) medium oatmeal	salt and pepper
½ lb (225 g) onions	water

Wash the stomach, inside and out, under a cold running tap. It should be used warty side out.

Chop the onions and suet finely. Mix all the ingredients together with enough water to make a slightly sloppy consistency. Fill into the skin, a bit more than half full. Tie or sew the skin up firmly, leaving enough slack for the meal to swell. Prick all over with a darning needle. Place in a pan of simmering water and boil for 2 hours. Remove from the water and cool. Slice and fry for breakfast or high tea.

Fruit Pudding

a sheep's stomach	3 oz (75 g) sugar
¾ lb (350 g) plain flour	a pinch of salt
6 oz (175 g) suet	mixed spice (optional—only in
a handful of raisins	moderation)

Wash the stomach as directed for the previous recipe. Chop the suet finely. Mix all the ingredients together with enough water to make a crumbly dough. Finish as for white pudding.

Black Pudding is the third of the local pudding trinity and the most popular of all. There is no point in giving directions, as it requires fresh sheep's blood. The local slaughter house will reserve the necessary when they kill anyone's sheep, so it is still commonly made at home in the Islands. It tastes quite different from English black pudding, which is made from pig's blood.

Marmalade

I hate making marmalade. When I'm shredding, I absent-mindedly put the pips in the peel bowl and vice versa. I forget how many pounds and how many pints before it comes to the cooking stage. I watch it for hours and it doesn't boil, then go away and leave it and it boils over. This year it boiled over to such effect that trickles of marmalade are still oozing out of crevices in the cooker 3 weeks later. And I don't even like the taste of it. Still, as marmalade goes, this is a good recipe, more fruity than some. It makes about 18 lb (8 kg).

    7 lb (2.2 kg) Seville oranges
    2 sweet oranges
    3 lemons
    14 pt (8.4 l) water
    12 lb (5.4 kg) sugar

Have ready a large bowl for the peel and a smaller one for the pips. Separate them as follows:

Cut each fruit in quarters. With a saw-edged knife, cut out the pips in a chunk. Most of the flesh will come too, but this doesn't matter. Put these chunks in the smaller bowl.

Shred the peel across in ¼-inch (6 mm) strips and put it in the other bowl.

Now cover both pips and peel with water, measuring the quantity you use, up to the full 14 pt (8.4 l). Leave for 24–48 hours.

Spread a square of muslin or a tea-towel in a sieve over a third bowl. Pour in the pips and their water. Tie up the cloth firmly, reserving the liquid that has gone through.

Now put that liquid, the bag of pips, the contents of the peel bowl and water to make up the 14 pt (8.4 l) into a jelly pan. Bring to the boil and simmer slowly till the peel is soft enough to break instantly at a pinch. This takes 1½–2 hours.

Remove the bag of pips, draining it well and returning the juice to the pan. Add the sugar and dissolve. Bring back to the boil and cook fairly rapidly till a little sets on a cold plate—the boiling temperature should be about 110°C/225°F. This will take a further ¾–2 hours, depending on how hard you boil it. Longer, slower cooking will produce a darker marmalade with a more barley-sugar flavour.

Remove the pan from the heat and take off any scum with a cold metal spoon. Allow the pan to stand for 15 minutes, then stir to distribute the peel evenly. Ladle into hot dry jars and cover.

You can use part muscovado sugar—about ⅓—if you like a slightly treacly flavour and a very dark colour. Be prepared for a much heavier scum and a poorer set though.

Thank goodness it only happens once a year.

Baking and Suchlike

"She wadna bake and she wadna brew
  Nickety, nackety, noo, noo, noo,
For fear o' spoilin' her gentle hue . . ."

That was the wife of the wee cooper o' Fife. Perhaps her stove was like mine. My oven is deep and my arms are short, and much-branded with incautious groping into the dark recesses. When the wind blows, as it usually does, the hot-plate glows orange, and my face cooks as much as my pancakes.

Everything baked that we use in the hotel is home-baked, with the exception of one item, of which more later. Fortunately, Harris women are wonderful bakers, and I have ducked out of many baking jobs which I would otherwise make a mess of, as I tend to forget about things in ovens till they start smoking. Many of the recipes in this section are with grateful acknowledgements to friends who bake for me.

Yeast Doughs

There is a misplaced mystique about breadmaking. It is really very easy, and needn't be time-consuming. You don't have to knead the stuff till your back is breaking and you don't need to let it rise twice—these are left-overs from the days of huge troughs of dough and home-cultured yeasts, when producing an even texture took both skill and muscle. You needn't hover over the dough while it rises: give it

½ an hour by a steaming saucepan, 2 hours in a not very warm kitchen, or overnight in the fridge, depending on what suits you.

Here are a few hints for the baker who has tried and failed:

(1) Have your yeast mixture nicely warm, but *never* uncomfortably hot.

(2) Don't make your dough too dry. It should be soft like scones or suet-crust, not firm like short pastry.

(3) Cover the rising dough with a damp tea-towel. If the top dries and hardens it will prevent the rest from rising.

(4) Don't rest the dough-filled tins on a very hot surface, or the bottom will harden before it can rise.

Flour

For most doughs, I use stoneground organic wholewheat bread-flour finely milled. Some organic wholewheat flours are "soft", i.e. low gluten, and make very dense bread. They are not always labelled, so it may take a bad experience or so before you learn what is what. A finely ground flour rises more easily than a coarse one, anyway. It is also a better bet for all-purpose cooking: you can use it for sauces, sponges and pastry, even though it is ostensibly for bread. If you are using wholewheat flour all the time, you may find it worth while buying a sack from a wholefood shop or wholesaler. Buy 100% wholewheat or wholemeal. "Wheatmeal" has had the bran removed.

For white bread, use only strong white flour. Unbleached has a slightly better flavour. Strong white flour tends to toughen sponges and pastry, but it is good for batters and not noticeable in sauces.

Other flours, such as oat and rye, are low gluten, so if you want a well-risen bread, you should use at least ¼ weight of hard wheat flour. But a dense un-British bread can be very good.

Yeast

Three kinds of yeast are generally available:

(1) Fresh yeast. This usually comes in a compressed block. You need 2 oz (50 g) for 3 lb (or a 1½ kilo bag) of flour. Mash it with 1 teaspoon of sugar till it goes runny. Add a cupful of the warm water required for the recipe and leave it till it foams. Add the rest of the liquid and proceed.

(2) Dried yeast. This is granulated. Use 1 oz (25 g) for 3 lb (1.5 kg)

flour. Sprinkle it into the warm liquid with 1 teaspoon of sugar, stir, and leave till it goes frothy.

(3) Instant yeast. This is almost a powder. Use 1 oz (25 g) for 3 lb (1.5 kg) flour, or a sachet as directed. Mix it into the flour, *not* into the liquid.

Don't be fooled by the apparently wholesome lack of sugar in type 3: instant yeast is encouraged to perform by various chemicals, which you can read about in the small print under the pretty picture. For the other types, sugar is just a convenient quick "food" to get them started. It is not absolutely necessary, and you certainly don't need the tablespoon or more recommended in many recipes, unless you like the taste. It's worth noting that large quantities of sugar, salt, melted fat or oil all inhibit the action of yeast. Certain fancy doughs containing these can be alarmingly slow to work, but will get there in the end.

All breads freeze reasonably well in the short term. Freshen them up by crisping the crust for 5 minutes in a moderate oven. After a week in the freezer, though, yeast doughs become progressively more crumbly.

Wholemeal Bread or Rolls

This quantity makes 3 loaves or 36 rolls.

> 2 oz (50 g) fresh yeast *or* 1 oz (25 g)
>   dried yeast
> 1 teaspoon sugar
> 1½ pt (825 ml) warm water
> 3–3¼ lb (1.4–1.5 kg) wholemeal
>   flour
> 1 level tablespoon salt

Treat the yeast as directed in the general remarks. Mix everything together and knead till coherent and elastic. Divide between greased loaf tins or make small balls, placed ½ inch (1.25 cm) apart on greased baking trays. Cover with a damp tea-towel and leave, out of draughts, till doubled in bulk. Bake in a hot oven—30–40 minutes for loaves 10–15 for rolls.

Test for readiness by poking the bottom. If it retains your fingerprint, give it another 5 minutes.

Jack MacWilliam's Wholemeal Bread

Jack's superb bread cuts and keeps much better than the basic recipe above. He bakes me 6 loaves every week and we use them for packed lunches and breakfast toast. It is so good that it takes an inhuman amount of will-power not to gobble any leftover toast that comes back to the kitchen immediately.

    1 tablespoon cooking oil
    1 flat tablespoon malt extract
    ¼ pt (150 ml) boiling water
    50 mg vitamin C (this is a yeast
       accelerator)
    1 flat tablespoon salt
    1¼ pt (700 ml) lukewarm water
    2 sachets instant yeast
    3¼ lb (1.5 kg) wholemeal flour

Stir the malt and oil into the boiling water, till well mixed. Crush the vitamin C tablets and salt and dissolve in the lukewarm water. Mix the yeast into the flour.

Pour the liquids into the flour and knead well. You may need up to ¼ pt (150 ml) extra of warm water.

Form into 3 loaves and leave to double in bulk. Bake in a hot oven—about 40 minutes.

Butteries

Butteries are a wondrous speciality of Aberdeen and the surrounding district, a relation of the French croissant. When I was a girl, every little bakery, of which there were many, had its own jealously-guarded recipe, and its own passionately loyal customers. Some bakers added a little sugar, some a splash of vinegar. Some used fat or milk in the basic dough. Some rolled thin, others squat. Some baked brown and crisp, others light gold and melting. We called these articles simply "rolls", judging no other bread worthy of the name, and they arrived in a paper bag on the doorstep, warm and fragrant, before 8 o'clock. They were considered stale by lunchtime. Not any more, I'm sorry to say; except in a very few country bakeries the modern version is flabby, coarse and cellophane-packed. Perhaps it is just as well: I fear my consistently ample girth is a consequence of an early addiction to these delectable pastries.

The simplest way to make these is to separate off a third of a batch of ordinary white bread dough and proceed from the first rolling. If the dough is too warm, it will be difficult to roll, so do this on a cold surface. If your butter is soft, spread it onto the dough as you would spread a slice of bread. If it is very cold, or better still frozen, grate it on a coarse grater. These methods are both much quicker than pinching off tiny pieces to cover the surface.

1 lb (450 g) strong white flour
1 teaspoon salt
½ oz (15 g) dried yeast *or* 1 oz
    (25 g) fresh
1 teaspoon sugar
½ pt (275 ml) lukewarm water
6–8 oz (175–225 g) butter or
    mixed butter and other fat
extra ½ oz (15 g) butter for the
    tops.

Treat the yeast according to the general directions. Mix the flour and salt. You can rub in 2 oz (50 g) of the fat if you want a very tender crumb.

Pour the yeast liquid into the flour and knead till smooth and silky. Cover with a tea-towel and leave in a warm place till double in bulk. Knead again. (This first rising is not essential, but it is an improvement. It makes the dough easier to roll.)

Roll the dough out on a floured cold surface, about ¼ inch (6 mm) thick. Starting from the left, dot ⅔ of the surface of the dough with ⅓ of the fat. Fold the right hand side over the middle section and the left hand side over that. Crimp down the edges and give the dough a half turn, so that the right hand fold now faces you.

Repeat this rolling, spreading and folding twice more, and if there are streaks of butter coming to the surface, do it again.

Now roll out about ¼ inch (6 mm) thick. Cut into about 12 rectangles. Fold the corners underneath and flatten slightly. Place on a baking tray, leaving ½ inch (1.25 cm) between to allow for spreading. Pinch the extra ½ oz (15 g) butter into flakes and put 1 on the top of each buttery. Put the tray in a warm place till they are well-risen and puffy looking, but don't give them so much heat that the butter melts and escapes.

Bake in a moderately hot oven for 10–15 minutes. When you take them out, spoon any fat which has run out back over the butteries, and leave to cool on the baking tray.

Oatmeal Bread or Rolls

This is a pleasant change from wheat bread. The rolls are very good
warm for breakfast. This quantity makes about 30.

> 2 lb (900 g) fine oatmeal
> 2 teaspoons salt
> 1¼ pt (700 ml) warm water
> 2 oz (50 g) fresh yeast *or* 1 oz (25 g)
>   dried yeast
> 1 teaspoon sugar
> ½ lb (225 g) wholemeal flour

Mix the oatmeal and salt with 1 pt (570 ml) warm water (1¼ pt
(700 ml) if you are going to use instant yeast). Leave to stand in a warm
place for 1 hour.

Treat the yeast as directed in the general instructions, using the other
¼ pt (150 ml) water unless it is the instant type. Add it to the oatmeal
with the wheat flour.

Mix thoroughly. It will be very sticky, so use only one hand at first.
Add some extra flour if it is too intractable, but this dough remains
rather soft. Form into loaves or rolls and leave covered with a damp
cloth. It takes a little longer to double in bulk than an all-wheat bread.
Bake as for wholemeal bread.

Afternoon Tea

Many innocuous people have a dream of driving on a lovely sunny
afternoon to a country retreat, there to drink tea out of pretty cups and
to consume fresh scones and home-made jam, with other delights.
Some of them still come hopefully to our door. Sometimes there is no
answer, if we have seen them coming and bolted up the hill. Sometimes
they find me in my gumboots, with a bucket of potatoes, and ill-
tempered. Sometimes they are greeted by our small grimy daughter and
her equally unclean friends. Sometimes they are molested by our hens,
who peck their toes if they are wearing sandals. Whatever happens,
they don't get any tea. This is extremely mean of us, but between 2 and
4 in the afternoon, the sight of a prospective guest is as a crucifix to a
vampire.

Come 4.30, we bow to the inevitable and concede (grudgingly) that
residents at least have to be allowed tea. Some of them are in a pitiable

state by then. They have motored all round the island looking for a pub to have lunch at, or walked 5 miles to the nearest shop only to discover it's Sunday.

Tea is unelaborate but elegant, with a silver tea-service, pink cups, warm scones and home-made jam, and cream if there is cream to spare. It is really better if there is no cream, as people always eat it and then feel bilious at dinner time.

Pancakes

Known as dropped scones or Scotch pancakes outside Scotland. Syrup makes them a more even brown than sugar, and sour milk gives a lighter result than fresh. The lightest and most velvety brown I have ever encountered were Mrs Peggy Macaskill's. She advised using water rather than milk.

> 4 oz (100 g) self-raising flour
> pinch of salt
> 2 teaspoons syrup *or* caster sugar
> 1 egg
> about ¼ pt (150 ml) milk, thick
>   sour milk if possible

Sift the flour and salt. Drop in the egg, the syrup or sugar, and half the milk. Beat hard till the mixture is smooth. Add more milk to make a thick batter and beat again till bubbles form. If there is time, let the batter stand for half an hour.

Heat a heavy frying pan till very hot—it should sizzle when you grease it. Don't over-grease: wipe the fat off again till the pan just shines.

Drop tablespoons of the batter on to the hot surface. As soon as bubbles rise and break, flip the pancakes over. They will only take seconds for the other side.

Keep them folded in a clean cloth till they have cooled, and use the same day.

Scones

Every housewife in the Hebrides has her own ways of making scones. Some leave them plain, others sweeten with syrup or sugar. Most people pat lightly rather than roll, and cut the dough into wedges or rectangles rather than rounds. Tops are left attractively floury, not glazed. I have collected these recipes from three of our helpers, but I never get as good results as they do.

Morag Macleod's Scones

Use sour milk for the best taste and lightest texture.

> 1 lb (450 g) self-raising flour
> ½ level teaspoon cream of tartar
> ½ level teaspoon bicarbonate of
> soda
> 2 oz (50 g) sugar
> 3 oz (75 g) margarine
> 2 eggs
> milk to mix—sour if possible

Add cream of tartar and bicarbonate of soda to the flour and rub in the margarine. Mix in the sugar. Stir in the beaten eggs and enough milk to make a soft dough.

Do not knead the dough. The less handling it gets the better the scones. Roll out gently ½ inch (1.25 cm) thick. Cut into pieces and bake about 15 minutes in a hot oven.

Mary Ann Macsween's Scones

> 2 lb (900 g) self-raising flour
> ½ teacup sugar
> 2 oz (50 g) margarine
> 1 tablespoon syrup or treacle
> 2 eggs
> about ¾ pt (425 ml) milk

Mix the flour and sugar and rub in the margarine. Add the syrup, eggs and enough milk to make a soft dough. Pat out very lightly about ½ inch (1.25 cm) thick. Cut into oblongs and bake in a very hot oven till well risen and golden brown—about 10 minutes.

Kathleen Morrison's Wholemeal Scones

8 oz (225 g) plain flour	a pinch of salt
8 oz (225 g) wholemeal flour	4 oz (100 g) margarine
1 level teaspoon bicarbonate of soda	2 oz (50 g) sugar
2 level teaspoons cream of tartar	1 egg
	milk to mix

Sieve the plain flour with the bicarbonate of soda, the cream of tartar, and the salt. Add the wholemeal flour and mix well. Rub in the margarine and add the sugar.

Beat the egg with a little milk and mix into the dry ingredients with a knife. (Don't use too much milk—this is a slightly drier dough than the other recipes given here.)

Turn onto a board floured with wholemeal. Knead lightly into a round. Cut into 8 or 10 wedges and bake in a hot oven till golden brown—10–15 minutes.

Victoria Plum Jam

My mother makes all the jam we use. This one is my favourite, excellent for tarts and sponges as well as on scones.
Makes about 12–14 lb (5.5–6.5 kg).

7 lb (3.2 kg) Victoria plums
7 lb (3.2 kg) sugar
½ pt (275 ml) water

Remove the stems from the plums. Rinse and drain them. Slit them down one side—this helps to free the stones on cooking. Put them in a pan with the water and cook gently till they are soft and the skins are tender.

Take out some of the stones and crack them with a hammer. Reserve the kernels.

Add the sugar to the plums and continue cooking, stirring till the sugar dissolves. Boil fairly hard for 20–25 minutes, till a little sets on a cold plate. Add the kernels to the boiling jam a few minutes before the end of the cooking time.

Take off any scum—a cold metal spoon is best for this. Remove the stones (they will mostly have risen to the top). Pour the jam into hot dry jars and cover.

Oatcakes

There are as many oatcake and bannock recipes in the Western Isles as there are grannies and aunties. The best are often made by octogenarians or even nonagenarians. I hasten to add that neither of the ladies who contributed these recipes is in that group yet.

Some people melt the fat, put in more raising agent or omit it altogether. Others add flour, to make handling easier, or sugar and extra fat to produce a more biscuity texture. Any type of oatcake can be cooked entirely in the oven, without using a girdle, or the first side can be done on the girdle and the drying out in the oven. The one feature common to all Hebridean oatcakes is their hefty thickness: elsewhere they are usually made thin and crisp. I remember years ago taking a present of oatcakes I had made to an elderly Harris lady. I had made them Aberdeen style—with melted dripping and not more than ⅛-inch (3 mm) thick. She eyed them with disapproval, and half an hour's conversation could not persuade her I had really intended to produce wretched things like that.

We always keep oatcakes for breakfast and to serve with cheese after dinner. Usually Morag makes them; if I do them myself, I forget my early training and use Joni's recipe.

Morag Macleod's Oatcakes

> 1 lb (450 g) oatmeal
> 6 oz (175 g) self-raising flour
> ½ teaspoon bicarbonate of soda
> 5½ oz (165 g) margarine
> ½ pt (275 ml) warm water

Mix all the dry ingredients together. Rub in the margarine till it resembles breadcrumbs. Add warm water and mix with your hand till it forms a stiffish dough. You may need a little extra water—if it is too dry it will crack on rolling out.

Put the dough onto an oatmeal-floured surface, form it into a ball, and roll it out about ½ inch (1.25 cm) thick. Do all this without a pause, as once the dough cools it will become dry and difficult to work.

Cut into oblongs and bake in a moderately hot oven for 20–30 minutes. The oatcakes should look pale and dry when they are done.

Joni Wilson's Oatcakes

1 lb (450 g) fine oatmeal
½ teaspoon bicarbonate of soda
pinch of salt
4–5 oz (100–150 g) margarine
1½–2 tablespoons hot water

Rub the fat into the dry ingredients till it sticks together. Add the hot water, enough to make it hold together in one lump, but don't make it soggy. Pat out ¼ inch (6 mm) thick, either in several 7-inch (17.5 cm) rounds or in one sheet. Cut into triangles if you made rounds or oblongs if you didn't. Bake on a greased girdle till they go firm, then transfer carefully to a baking tray. Dry them off in a moderate oven for about 15 minutes. Don't let them burn.

Other Savoury Biscuits

Morag's oatcakes made me ashamed of the bought crackers offered alongside them with cheese, so I evolved the next two recipes last season. Unfortunately, they were so popular that I spent half the day baking more and more of them, and by the middle of the summer I had run out of enthusiasm for it.

If you don't care for sweet biscuits, try these instead; they don't need cheese or butter.

Caraway Biscuits

10 oz (275 g) plain flour
½ teaspoon salt
1 teaspoon caster sugar
1–2 teaspoons caraway seeds
1 teaspoon ground coriander or
   grated lemon rind
6 oz (175 g) butter

Rub the fat into the dry ingredients till you have a cohesive dough like shortbread. Roll out ⅛ inch (3 mm) thick. Cut into rounds and bake in a moderate oven till pale golden—10–15 minutes.

Stripey Biscuits

8 oz (225 g) wholemeal flour
1 level teaspoon baking powder
a large pinch sugar
a large pinch salt
4 oz (100 g) butter or margarine
3 egg yolks
2 tablespoons sesame seeds
2 tablespoons poppy seeds

Mix the dry ingredients except the seeds, and rub in the fat. When the mixture begins to stick together, bind it with the beaten egg yolks.

Keep back a little egg yolk and mix it with a teaspoon of water. This is for glazing.

Roll out the dough about ⅛ inch (3 mm) thick, as near an oblong as possible. Push and trim it to square it off. Brush the whole surface with the egg glaze.

Sprinkle the 2 kinds of seed in alternate stripes across the dough. Cut into fingers at right angles to the stripes. Be careful lifting them onto the baking tray as they lose the seeds easily. Bake in a moderate oven for 10–15 minutes.

Lena Maclennan's Shortbread Biscuits

These are to be found in the tins on the bedroom tea-trays. They are one of the greatest delicacies of the house. I have discerned meek and law-abiding guests smuggling them into their cars; the tin of many a dieting lady has been found mysteriously empty by evening; penniless honeymooners who couldn't afford dinner have lived on these and love. On Lena's baking day, a procession of assorted children and dogs (only three of each, but it seems like more) trots between her kitchen and mine, bearing empty and full tins in expectation of fragrant rewards fresh from her oven.

2 teacups plain flour
1 teacup cornflour
1 teacup icing sugar
½ lb (225 g) butter

Rub all the ingredients together into a firm dough. Roll out thinly (⅛ inch (3 mm)). Cut into small rounds and bake in a moderate oven till crisp and golden—10–15 minutes.

Pat MacWilliam's Rich Fruit Cake

Pat is the other half of the one who makes the bread. This rich, moist cake embellishes packed lunches. It is good eaten at once and even better after a few weeks' maturation. I think the specially fruity taste comes from Pat's home-candied peel, so I include the recipe below.

10 oz (275 g) butter	1½ lb (675 g) currants
10 oz (275 g) caster sugar	6 oz (175 g) candied peel
7–8 eggs	4 oz (100 g) almonds
14 oz (400 g) plain flour	4 oz (100 g) glacé cherries
1 dessertspoon mixed spice	grated rind of 1 lemon
a pinch of salt	juice of ½ lemon

Preheat oven to 160°C/325°F. Line a deep 8–9 inch (20–22.5 cm) round tin.

Sieve the flour with the spice and salt. Pick over the currants. Chop the peel, cherries and almonds.

Cream the butter and sugar till light. Beat in the eggs one by one. Add the flour mixture alternately with the fruit. Mix in the lemon rind and juice.

Turn the mixture into the prepared tin. Bake in a slow oven for 1½ hours, then reduce heat to very slow and bake a further 2 hours. Turn off the oven and leave the cake in for a further 15 minutes.

Candied Peel

8 oz (225 g) orange and lemon peel
8 oz (225 g) granulated sugar
½ pt (275 ml) water

Remove loose pith from the peel, as you use the fruit. Save the peel in the freezer till you have enough. Chop it, pour boiling water over it and leave it overnight.

Drain off the water. Cover with fresh cold water, bring to the boil and simmer till tender—at least 20 minutes. Drain.

Put the sugar in a pan with ½ pt (275 ml) water. Dissolve and bring to the boil. Add the peel and simmer till the syrup is almost absorbed. Cool and pack in plastic bags or cartons.

Sweets

One Christmas when we were very hard up I solved the present problem by giving everyone home-made sweets. For days on end I hung over boiling syrups, beat fudge, worked fondant, pulled Edinburgh Rock and dipped chocolates. The Turkish Delight bounced, the brittle deliquesced, and the chocolates dulled. I burnt the bottoms out of 2 saucepans and most of the skin off my fingers. Since then I have refused to have anything to do with confectionery.

Marzipan

Even Andrew can make this without instruction. It keeps very well in a box in the fridge.

> ½ lb (225 g) ground almonds
> ½ lb (225 g) caster sugar
> 1 large egg
> 1 tablespoon of any fruit liqueur
>   (you can also use rum, sherry or
>   rosewater)

Mix all the ingredients to a putty-like consistency. If it is too sticky, add more almonds and sugar. Pinch off small balls and decorate with nuts.
    You can also use this to stuff dates and cover Christmas cakes.

Pat MacWilliam's Fudge

Don't be incredulous about the quantity of vanilla essence. The butter offsets it—very good indeed.

> 1 lb (450 g) pale soft brown sugar
> 1 large tin condensed milk
> ½ lb (225 g) butter
> 1 tablespoon milk
> 1 dessertspoon vanilla essence

Put everything but the vanilla essence in a heavy pan. Heat slowly till the sugar dissolves, stirring all the time. Bring to the boil, still stirring. Boil for 15 minutes—keep stirring. Beat slightly, stir in the vanilla essence, beat again. Pour into a greased Swiss Roll tin. Mark into squares before it is cold.

Soft Cheeses

We usually serve one or two fresh soft cheeses after dinner, for those who are daunted by the venerable aspect of the Stilton and its colleagues.

Yoghurt Cheese in Oatmeal

Yoghurt cheese is excellent for cheesecakes or any recipe that calls for curd or quark. The whey is nutritious too—very good for hens.

 1 pt (570 ml) yoghurt
 2 tablespoons pinhead oatmeal

Line a sieve with muslin and set it over a bowl. Put in the yoghurt and drain for at least 6 hours. Salt the curd if you want to, and roll it gently into a sausage inside its muslin. Put the oatmeal on a flat plate (pinhead, the coarsest, is best). Roll the curd out onto the oatmeal and scoop more meal over it. Keep it in the fridge till you are ready to serve it. Use within 24 hours.

Crowdie and Cream

Well! Here it is at last—the food that Finlay J. Macdonald has made Scarista famous for. Quite likely you only bought my book because of his *Crowdie and Cream*. No one can better describe this traditional delight than Finlay: "Once the cream had been removed, gallons of thick sour milk were left over every week, and the sour milk, when it was stood on a warm fire, converted into crowdie, which floated to the surface of tangy, refreshing whey—the ideal drink for hot days of peat-cutting or haymaking. . . . But the greatest delicacy of them all was the crumbly crowdie mixed with fresh cream, which piled high on a fresh oatcake, spread with fresh butter, combined into a flavour with an inbuilt memory. Crowdie and cream! The bitter and the sweet blending. . . ."*

As you can gather from this, crowdie is usually made from the skimmed milk left after the cream has been taken off to make butter, but you can use whole milk. Pasteurised milk is unlikely to work, though: it turns thin and putrid, not thick and sour. Mary MacDonald,

* *Crowdie and Cream* by Finlay J. MacDonald (Macdonald & Co, 1982).

the Scarista postmistress, often gives me a present of some crowdie, and it is her method I give below. The basic crowdie freezes very well, she tells me, but don't add the salt and cream till you are ready to use it.

8 pt (4.6 l) skimmed milk
salt
double cream

Leave the milk in a warm place to sour and thicken. Now stand it on a very, very low heat. If you have a solid fuel stove, the hottest part of the top other than the cooking area is ideal. Leave it overnight. If you can't manage such a low heat, use the lowest you can for several hours. The milk will separate into curds and whey—Mary says it is best when the curd sinks, which it doesn't always do. Drain off the whey.

To serve, mash some crowdie with a little salt and add cream to taste—I find about 3 tablespoonfuls to 4 oz (100 g) cheese is right.

You can add chopped chives or other fresh herbs to crowdie. It isn't authentic, but it makes a pleasant change.

Some Dinner Menus

Mostly you will have your own ideas about dinner parties. Personally, I have never been able to use the menu sections at the back of cookery books. During my cooking life, I have always been without at least one of the essentials they tend to assume: cash—an oven—shops—and where on earth do you find lengkuas root?

The present menus are no more resourceful, but perhaps some well-organised hosts and hostesses will manage to use them. They are in the Scarista House style, but rather simpler, as when I am cooking for hotel guests I don't have to sit at table with them and make light conversation while the kitchen burns down.

A few hints:

(1) Plan your party according to the season. No use having the cash, the oven, the shops—even the lengkuas root—and then discovering there's no asparagus till next May.

(2) Pay attention to colour and texture, as well as taste. Don't have red soup followed by red gravy, or a savoury and a sweet mousse at the same meal. If you get caught out, seize a few green leaves for colour or some chopped nuts for texture to vary the effect.

(3) Food is meant to nourish. Don't overcook everything or keep it warm for ages: better to stick to a simpler meal with some cold items that can be ready before your guests arrive. And don't stuff them silly: cream and egg yolks with everything and pie followed by pie may seem mouthwatering when you're feeling ravenous as you plan your dinner, but by half way through the meal it will become a pain in some part or other of everyone's anatomy.

These menus are arranged in twos—a fish and a meat main course for each part of the year.* Underneath is a vegetarian main dish which can be fitted in to either menu.

Without injury to the balance of the meal, you can scrap the pudding and serve whatever fruit and/or cheese is good at the time. Don't forget celery, radishes, figs, dates and nuts, all of which make a leisurely and convivial ending to a meal, if you don't want to bother with a sweet. Pass the port, please.

Spring

1. Nettle Soup

   Liver with Sage and Orange
   Spaghetti
   Steamed Carrots

   Caramel Mousse

   Wine: Gamay de l'Ardèche
   or red Sancerre

2. Grapefruit Water Ice

   Mussels with Fennel
   Oatmeal Rolls
   Salad

   Hot Chocolate Pudding

   Wine: Muscadet

Vegetarian alternative: Courgettes with cheese

Early Summer

1. Borshcht

   Stuffed Shoulder of Lamb
   Fresh Mint Sauce
   Potatoes with Rosemary
   Spring Cabbage

   Hazelnut Meringue Cake

   Wine: full-bodied claret,
   e.g. Cissac

2. Cauliflower Soufflés

   Baked Salmon with Raita
   New Potatoes
   Courgettes with Tomato
     Sauce

   Butterscotch Ice Cream

   Wine: Vouvray or Montlouis

Vegetarian alternative: Spicy Stuffed Tomatoes

---

* I have given wine suggestions. If you notice a preponderance of Loire and Rhône wines and wonder why, write to Robin Yapp for elucidation. One of his recent lists was mainly in classical Greek so it may not elucidate everything. Address at the back of the book.

Late Summer

1. Avocado and Walnut Salad

   Venison Pie
   Julienne of Celery and Potato

   Summer Trifle

   Wine: red Rhône, e.g.
         Châteauneuf du Pape

2. Melon with Blackcurrant Water
   Ice

   Scallops in Oatmeal
   Spicy Tomato Sauce
   Carrot and Potato Cake

   Almond Cake with Peaches

   Wine: Sancerre

Vegetarian alternative: Spinach Soufflé Flan

Autumn

1. Pepper Fritters and Tomato
   Granita

   Lamb with Apricots
   Rice with Pine Kernels
   Steamed Calabrese

   Syllabub

   Wine: Rioja, e.g. Vina Ardanza

2. Apple-stuffed Mushrooms

   Turbot with Dill Sauce
   Burghul Pilaff
   Colourful Mixed Salad

   Queen of Puddings

   Wine: white burgundy,
         e.g Meursault

Vegetarian alternative: Aubergine Pizza

Winter

1. Carrot and Orange Soup

   Pot-roasted Pheasant
   Skirlie Potatoes
   Lemon Cabbage

   Bananas Flambées

   Wine: light burgundy,
         e.g. Fleurie, Rully

2. Curd Cheese Ramekins

   Halibut with Mushrooms
   Buckwheat with Cucumber
   Casserole of Sweet Peppers

   Chocolate Chestnut Cake

   Wine: dry rosé, e.g. Tavel or
         Sancerre

Vegetarian alternative: Gougère of Mushrooms and Peppers

How Carnivores Can Cope
with Vegetarians

It is becoming increasingly common for people who are not vegetarians themselves to be faced with the problem of catering for vegetarians. So if you are a parent of alternative offspring or a police officer with the cells full of ALF detainees, read on.

The chances are your charges will be vegans. This means you have to forget about the "We can always give them cheese or eggs" theory. Vegans do not eat anything of animal origin, so dairy produce, eggs and honey are debarred. You will have two headaches: how to provide enough daily protein, and how to produce variety.

Take the protein question first. It is worth remembering that in Britain and America we eat far more protein than we need, on average. Particularly for adults, it is not necessary or even healthy to consume large quantities of concentrated animal protein—meat, fish, eggs, cheese and milk. Still less do we need animal fats—certainly not two or three times a day.

> "Breakfast, Dinner, Lunch and Tea
>   Are all the human frame requires",

concluded Henry King, who chewed Bits of String, and was Early cut off in Dreadful Agonies. But he could have been wrong. If he had stuck to string and missed out the bacon and egg, roast beef, fried mutton chops, iced cakes and buttered scones, he might have been alive and well, albeit, like most vegans, lanky. For the secrets of vegan eating are the proteins, vitamins and trace minerals in unrefined carbohydrate foods. All whole grains, pulses and nuts and the flours and pastes made from them provide satisfactory nourishment. Furthermore, if you eat a grain and a pulse at the same meal (not necessarily cooked together), the proteins are better utilised by the body. Ethnic food all over the world shows instinctive understanding of this fact—peanuts with millet, lentils with rice, beans with pasta, sesame paste with pitta bread. Reckon on a combined dry weight of 4–6 oz (100–175 g) per serving for a satisfying meal. Sprouting seeds such as mung and alfalfa are also nutritious. Raw and cooked fruit and vegetables are as good for vegans as for everyone else, but it is even more important not to peel or overcook everything, as these practices are a great waste of nourishment and a sure way of cementing up your innards.

So much for the serious business of nourishment. But what about enjoyment? Endless bowls of brown rice and lentils imply a dismal monotony. But have a browse through the ethnic recipe books which are on sale everywhere nowadays, particularly from Middle Eastern and Indian cuisine, and you will get plenty of ideas for gingering up the basic grain/pulse combination (lengkuas root?). One visit to a Pakistani grocer or a delicatessen should arm you with sufficient spices, condiments and oils to keep you experimenting for months. By that time your pestilent teenager will have taken up some other fad anyway, but who knows, you may have got a taste for the stuff yourself.

Remember that a vegan diet is perfectly acceptable to any vegetarian, but not vice versa, so if in doubt cook vegan. Particularly, vegetarians who are so for humane reasons will be revolted by non-free-range eggs. Anyway, vegetarians are bedevilled by cheese omelettes, which everyone from best friend to expense-account restaurant thinks are very good for them, and you will win esteem and affection by giving them a nice plate of beans instead.

Whether you are dealing with vegans or other vegetarians, if you have to provide more than just the occasional meal, avoid two pitfalls. Keep clear of processed foods, particularly if your vegetarian is rigorous. On the whole (the exceptions are usually confined to healthfood shops) such foods contain meat by-products, animal fats, battery eggs—quite likely hoof-and-horn meal, under some long chemical name. By the time you have read the labels carefully, you might as well have bought raw ingredients and made it yourself. The other mistake to avoid is always sticking to traditional English-style cooking, substituting lentils (say) for meat and vegetable margarine for lard or butter. This can produce very heavy and greasy results, and very fattening too. When I was at university in Aberdeen, the local bakers' answer to vegetarians (there weren't many, and I wasn't one of them) was a macaroni pie—a pie shell made with white flour, filled with white pasta in cheese sauce, with a lid of mashed potato on top. There was a baked bean version too: indeed they are both still around, and can fill a gap in a hungry student, but the general principle is not healthy. Refined carbohydrates, such as white flour, soak up any amount of fat, and lack proper nutrients. The end result is stodgy and unwholesome. I am reminded of some guests we once had, who had, they assured us, taken to a high-fibre diet—then newly the rage. But they had to abandon it because they gained so much weight: "It was all the baked beans we had to eat," they explained. Well! the beans may have been fibrous before they got in the tin, but by the time they are eaten, the fibres have swelled to saturation point, permeating them with an unholy solution of white sugar, white flour, water and vinegar. So go easy on the macaroni and chips and the baked bean crumble. Use *whole* foods —warts and all.

Some Useful Addresses

For information on factory farming and how to combat it:
        Compassion in World Farming,
        20 Lavant Street,
        Petersfield,
        Hants GU32 3EW
        Tel. Petersfield (0730) 64208

For a helpful list of stockists if you have trouble getting hold of free range eggs:
        Free Range Egg Association (FREGG),
        37 Tanza Road,
        London NW3 2UA
        Tel. (01) 435 2596

For free range pork, ham and sausages (mail order and callers):
        Anne Petch,
        Heal Farm,
        King's Nympton,
        Umberleigh,
        Devon EX37 9TB
        Tel. South Molton (07695) 2077

For non-intensively reared meat:
        Wholefood Butchers,
        31 Paddington Street,
        London W1
        Tel. (01) 486 1390

For non-intensively reared meat and organic fruit and vegetables:
>   Real Life Foods,
>   19 Maze Road,
>   Kew,
>   Richmond,
>   Surrey
>   Tel. (01) 940 5299

For Rhône and Loire wines (particularly good with the recipes in this book):
>   Yapp Bros.,
>   The Old Brewery,
>   Mere,
>   Wilts BA12 6DY
>   Tel. Mere (0747) 860423

If you suspect mislabelling of goods, e.g. that items marked "free range" are not, contact the Department of Consumer Protection at your local Council offices.

Index

A HOUSE BY THE SHORE
Twelve Years In The Hebrides
Alison Johnson

'The delightful story of an unlikely success in the farthest, wildest corner of the British Isles'
Daily Mail

The island of Harris is one of the most beautiful places in the world. The scenery is varied: steep and rugged mountains, misty crags and corries, sour peat bogs and sandy beaches .. a spectacular, sometimes eerie landscape.

To this remote corner of Scotland came Alison and Andrew Johnson, fleeing urban life. For months they lived on sheep's head broth and cabbage while they searched the island for a derelict old house to convert into a hotel. Then they discovered the old manse at Scarista, and fell in love.

But the object of their affections, focus of their almost impatient ambitions was almost a ruin. There were rats. Dead sheep. Windows, doors, floors needed replacing. And even after months of backbreaking work had created from this chaos a unique inn to match two extraordinary inn-keepers, there was no licence, and major problems with supplies.

But at last there was success, crowned by a visit from the Prince of Wales. A quite exceptional enterprise had come of age.

A HOUSE BY THE SHORE — a vivid description of a successful endeavour, and of the fascinating region and wild life, both animal and human, which provided both background and challenge.

'a book to take on holiday' *Glasgow Herald*

'highly readable' *Sunday Telegraph*

FUTURA PUBLICATIONS
NON-FICTION/AUTOBIOGRAPHY
0 7088 3404 3

THE NEW FISH COOKBOOK
Janet Horsley

FISH: fresh, filleted or fried in fingers; poached, potted or in a pie; smoked, steamed or stuffed; fish has become a favourite food. It's infinitely varied, amazingly versatile, tremendously good value, fashionable with the foodies — *and it's good for you!*

THE NEW FISH COOKBOOK is crammed with oceans of enticing recipes for every occasion: classic soups and stocks such as bouillabaisse with sauce rouille; exquisite hors d'oeuvre, perhaps smoked mussels in garlic butter or perfect potted shrimps; then spaghetti alla vongole John Dory with herbs, cider and cream or Filey's Good Friday pie ... The selection is so tempting — delicate crab souffle or saucy red mullet nicoise, squid with fresh ginger or Gloucester hake? Fish can be simple or sophisticated but it's always high in protein, low in cholesterol and delicious to eat.

Janet Horsley, who writes for the *Yorkshire Post*, tells all you need to know about the selection, preparation and cooking of over fifty different varieties of fish in a gourmet's odyssey from bloaters and brill to whelks and whiting.

FUTURA PUBLICATIONS
NON-FICTION/COOKERY
0 7088 3385 3

THE SALAD BOWL
Sonia Allison

Fresh, crunchy vegetables and fruit combined with cheese or pasta, seafood or poultry, together with a tangy dressing. Not just a treat for the tastebuds, but also a rich source of all the elements essential to a healthy diet.

In THE SALAD BOWL, there is something for everyone. You could start with appetizing Chestnut Cocktails, Crunchy Vegetarian Salad or Creamed Mushroom and Bacon Salad. Then on to savoury Marinaded Cucumber and Tarragon Salad, Madras Split Pea Salad or Special Eastern Turkey Salad. And of course something sweet to finish — maybe Gooseberry Puzzle Mould, Summer Glory Compote or refreshing Blueberry and Peach Salad.

Sonia Allison has devised almost two hundred delectable salad recipes and a variety of tasty dressings, using a wide range of unusual ingredients and seasonings as well as all the old favourites.

THE SALAD BOWL: a must for every kitchen.

FUTURA PUBLICATIONS
NON-FICTION/COOKERY
0 7088 3127 3

THAI COOKING
Jennifer Brennan

Thai cooking blends Chinese, Indian and Arabic influences into a unique cuisine. This is the first comprehensive and authentic book on Thai (Siamese) cooking and it brings the delicious secrets of Thai cuisine within the grasp of every cook.

A typical Thai dinner consists of an assortment of curry dishes, soups, salads, vegetables and sauces served simultaneously around a central bowl of plain boiled rice. Recipes range from *Quail Egg Flowers, Prawns caught In a Net* and *Bamboo Shoot and Pork Soup* to *Sweet and Sour Beef* and *Whole Fried Fish with Ginger Sauce*. The final chapters are dedicated to desserts and sweets — everything from *Thai Fried Bananas* to *Mangoes and Sticky Rice*.

'Sublimely varied, exciting, colourful and intensely delicious'
The Sunday Times

FUTURA PUBLICATIONS
NON-FICTION/COOKERY
0 7088 2555 9

CROCKPOT COOKING
Mary Norwak

Switch it on in the morning — and have a delicious meal ready in the evening — the crockpot could transform your life.

The crockpot — the combination of traditional cooking methods and modern technology ... an earthenware casserole which you just switch on before leaving for work. It cooks gently all day, using only the power needed for an electric light bulb. And you come home to a perfectly cooked meal.

The crockpot is economical, safe — there's no danger of boiling over, burning or cooking dry — and it preserves the flavours and nutritional values of foods.

Now bestselling cookery author Mary Norwak tells you all you need to know about crockpots — how to use and look after them, the best cooking methods for various foods and, of course, dozens of delicious recipes from soups, stews and fish, to jams and pickles.

FUTURA PUBLICATIONS
NON-FICTION/COOKERY
0 8600 7579 6

THE COMPLETE BOOK OF BARBECUES
Mary Norwak

Outdoor parties in the long summer evenings; the smell of wood smoke and charcoal fires; the fragrance of herbs and spit-roasted lamb — all these and more make up the charm of the barbecue.

Whether you're planning a barbecue party, a family feast or a quiet meal for two, Mary Norwak's THE COMPLETE BOOK OF BARBECUES is the perfect guide.

Mary Norwak provides all the practical information you need — types of barbecue, fire building, basic cooking rules and equipment — and a host of delicious recipes for main courses, sauces, marinades and dressings, from the simple but delicious hamburger to such gourmet delights as veal chops with kirsch, spiced orange glazed spare ribs, mussels and bacon and spit-roasted duck.

FUTURA PUBLICATIONS
NON-FICTION/COOKERY
0 8600 7209 6

All Futura Books are available at your bookshop or
newsagent, or can be ordered from the following address:
Futura Books, Cash Sales Department,
P.O. Box 11, Falmouth, Cornwall, TR10 9EN.

Please send cheque or postal order (no currency), and
allow 60p for postage and packing for the first book plus
25p for the second book and 15p for each additional book
ordered up to a maximum charge of £1.90 in U.K.

B.F.P.O. customers please allow 60p for the first book,
25p for the second book plus 15p per copy for the next
7 books, thereafter 9p per book.

Overseas customers, including Eire, please allow £1.25
for postage and packing for the first book, 75p for the second
book and 28p for each subsequent title ordered.